I   ET

a n   are

edited by Louis Nicholson
First Consulting Group

The INTERNET
and Healthcare

second edition

Health Administration Press
Chicago, Illinois

03   02   01   5   4   3

Library of Congress Cataloging-in-Publication Data

The Internet and healthcare / edited by Louis Nicholson. — 2nd ed.
    p. cm.
    Includes bibliographical references and index.
    ISBN 1-56793-097-2 (alk. paper)
    1. Health services administration—Computer network resources.   2. Internet (Computer network)   I. Nicholson, Louis.
    RA971.23.I56   1999
    362.1'0285'4678—dc21   98-48490
                                                   CIP

The paper used in this publication meets the minimum requirements of American National Standards for Information Sciences—Permanence of Paper for Printed Library Materials, ANSI Z39.48–1984. ♾ ™

Health Administration Press
A division of the Foundation of the
  American College of Healthcare Executives
One North Franklin Street
Chicago, IL 60606
312/424–2800

Table of Contents

Preface

Released in 1997, the first edition of this book aimed to improve healthcare delivery by teaching organizations how to harness the power of the Internet. In this second edition, we uphold that mission by keeping pace with the steady stream of changes and innovations that have occurred since the first edition was published.

To keep the information timely and accurate, we fast-tracked the revision process. We have reviewed, reaffirmed, and revitalized the chapters originally published, strengthening their relevance and value to today's healthcare organization. We have updated statistics to reflect growth and changes in Internet use, and we have amended or expanded charts and figures where needed.

In addition, we are introducing two new chapters that offer in-depth assessments of particular Internet applications and the ways they can enrich healthcare delivery. In Peter Kilbridge and Michael Schneider's "Implications of the Internet: The Physician's Perspective" and John Odden's "Call Centers and the Internet," the authors show why the Internet deserves its expanding reputation as a valuable business tool—not only for providers, but also for consumers.

As editor, I owe special thanks to Kent Gray and Briggs Pille for their dedication to making this second edition a richer book. Their efforts as reviewers and advisors were invaluable.

Kent and Briggs join with me to thank Peter Kilbridge, Michael Schneider, and John Odden for their new chapters, John Odden for updating the glossary, Judith Douglas for overseeing and expediting the revision process, and Jennifer Lillis, for copyediting and collaborating with our experts.

We also acknowledge the contributions of Jim Reep, who had the insight to understand the Internet's potential role in healthcare and shared that vision with those fortunate enough to be his colleagues.

Louis Nicholson

Introduction

The relationship between the Internet and the healthcare industry is not a new phenomenon. For years, physicians have been using the Internet to conduct research and confer with colleagues, while computer-savvy consumers have been using it to find information on health, fitness, prevention, disease, and medicine. It is estimated that more than 40 percent of the information found on the Internet today is related to healthcare.

What is new about the role of the Internet in healthcare is the Internet's transition from a communications medium for researchers to a powerful business tool that can play a significant role in reshaping the entire healthcare industry. The growing value of the Internet as a business tool lies along two powerful vectors.

The first vector is the Internet's ability to connect, in a standardized way, people and organizations that did not have such a capability in the past. The second vector is its standardized approach to communications among computer systems. Unlike the proprietary computer systems used by most businesses, Internet technology is based on a concept of openness that topples traditional barriers to sharing information across a network. Now, more people are connected to the network and can readily communicate using standardized and cost-effective tools.

The unification of these two powerful vectors has driven interest in the Internet, from academia to Wall Street to Main Street. This unification will enable innovative approaches to healthcare delivery, financing, and administration. It is inevitable that all the major healthcare industry stakeholders will begin using the Internet as the preferred method for collecting, disseminating, and sharing information.

Each of these stakeholders—purchasers, payors, hospitals, physicians, consumers, and regulators—is struggling to respond to the forces reshaping the healthcare industry, and naturally each is exerting pressure to mold the environment in favor of its own interests. New strategically oriented healthcare applications delivered on the Internet are beginning to flourish. Payors use the Internet to streamline their administrative processes and provide information to plan members. Providers use the Internet to share information and improve clinical and financial outcomes. Employers use the Internet to inform employees of benefits and provide access to health information. Patients use the Internet to become better-informed consumers of healthcare. As each sector of the healthcare industry responds to the forces reshaping the market, the Internet is playing an increasingly important role in recasting the delivery of healthcare.

This evolution toward the Internet in healthcare was spurred by the social, political, and economic costs of healthcare in the United States. In 1995, overall healthcare spending in the United States exceeded 15 percent of the gross domestic product (GDP). During this same period, other industrialized nations spent only 5 to 10 percent of their GDP on healthcare while achieving comparable levels of overall health status. In this high-cost environment, corporate profits and tax dollars are not the only concerns—U.S. global competitiveness is also at stake.

As a result, the industry has begun looking at information systems to support and streamline the delivery of healthcare. By tracking how and where healthcare dollars are being spent, industry stakeholders can minimize the hidden costs in excess, dubious, or repeat testing, treatment, diagnosis, and equipment. Hospitals have closed, and physicians have quit practice or become employees of large healthcare organizations. The phenomenal growth of managed care and the emergence of provider-sponsored networks illustrate that the old model of hospital-based, fee-for-service illness care is neither cost effective nor clinically efficient.

The restructuring of the healthcare system will have tremendous and complex implications for information management. The information systems and telecommunications strategy and requirements necessary for the restructured system are massive and will be expensive and complicated to implement. For example, the new integrated delivery system (IDS) models must support not only most of the classic managed care applications (e.g., member and contract management, product development), but also the additional systems that support the IDS infrastructure (e.g., network management, clinical and financial data repositories, clinic and office practice management, clinical and financial decision support) or that are unique to the delivery of patient care. Therefore, the new models of healthcare delivery are dependent on information technology, particularly because the measurement of these factors for decision making, as well as for the reengineering of business and clinical processes, depends on the immediate availability of current, accurate information.

As a result, many payors and providers are beginning to implement cost-effective, Internet-based solutions to improve the flow of information between organizations. IBM, Healtheon, and other technology vendors have begun working with several Blue Cross organizations and other health plans to develop Internet applications for payor-to-employer and payor-to-member electronic communications. These projects are designed to significantly reduce the costs of administrative paperwork while providing consumers with a better understanding of available healthcare benefits and options.

Information systems have become a requirement for hospitals as they grapple with the new clinical and financial requirements of managed care. IDSs are fueled by information. Winners in the IDS marketplace will be characterized by their ability to quickly gather and analyze clinical and financial data, make sound decisions, communicate new directions, and execute strategies. As healthcare enterprises become larger and are distributed over wider geographic regions, more emphasis will be placed on developing information systems that enable organizational communications and facilitate collaboration among financial and clinical managers responsible for delivering high-quality, cost-effective outcomes across different facilities.

Because of these trends, many hospitals and IDSs have substantially increased their capital spending on information technology (IT) from the traditional level of 2 to 3 percent of revenues to a much more substantial 5 or more percent. A growing percentage of this IT investment is being directed at Internet technologies that use network-based tools and applications to increase organizational communications, to streamline processes through electronic workflow improvement, and to leverage intellectual capital through the use of collaborative tools and databases.

Today, more and more healthcare organizations are turning to Internet-enabled information technologies, such as web interfaces like Lotus Domino and distribution tools like Marimba Castanet. The more aggressive organizations are developing applications (e.g., the Java programming language) based on Internet-driven technologies. Companies like Healtheon are developing innovative Java-based solutions that simplify support and reduce overall development time.

Payors and medical providers require significant information technology to capture, review, and disseminate administrative, financial, and clinical information. When organizations have information systems that can achieve the required level of administrative integration among payors, medical providers, employers, and consumers, they will be able to control costs while improving care delivery and enhancing patient satisfaction.

As valuable as the Internet has become for connecting all the players in the healthcare industry, the most potentially valuable applications are being developed for use within healthcare organizations. Intranets, which use the same tools and processes of the Internet but operate on an organization's private network, show great promise in providing new ways to improve communications, increase professional collaboration, and leverage intellectual capital through enhanced information sharing. As healthcare organizations consolidate into ever larger and more complex enterprises, these potent capabilities can enable managers to successfully leverage the two scarcest resources in the changing healthcare industry: knowledge and time.

Effective information systems are a critical success factor in enabling physicians to provide high-quality clinical outcomes at cost-effective rates. As a result of their need for timely, high-quality information, physicians have been among the first to make use of the Internet. An estimated 90 percent of all academic physicians and more than 25 percent of community physicians are frequent users of the Internet. Physicians have traditionally used the Internet to communicate with colleagues, obtain peer-reviewed articles, search medical databases, pursue continuing medical education (CME), and interact with relevant medical discussion groups. This trend will accelerate as physicians encounter the rising number of informed consumers obtaining medical information on the Internet.

The concept of the information-empowered patient is growing rapidly, and the days of "the doctor is always right" are receding. In the near future, it will not be uncommon for patients to supply their physicians with the latest in disease research and treatment information gathered from the Internet. Patients will expect physicians to be not only familiar with the research, but also prepared to comment on its applicability and provide fact-based explanations on why it should or should not be incorporated into the treatment plan.

Several Internet-based physician credential services are in development that will enable consumers to check the background, references, and quality indicators of individual physicians. Health plan and physician performance will undergo greater scrutiny as Health Plan Employer Data and Information Set (HEDIS) report cards and other quality indicators enable consumers to perform objective quality comparisons for the first time. Internet-based discussion groups and search engine capabilities will also enable consumers to both register complaints and seek out feedback from a broad array of individual and consumer watchdog resources.

Regulators and the accrediting bodies currently use the Internet to provide updates on their efforts. The National Committee for Quality Assurance (NCQA), for example, has as an active Internet site (www.ncqa.org) that distributes progress reports on HEDIS. In the future, regulators will be able to use the Internet to publish and disseminate information directly to consumer groups and others interested in keeping tabs on health plans and medical providers.

As these forces interact and combine with each other in the healthcare marketplace, an entirely new and highly competitive industry will emerge. In this new environment, the Internet will help

- medical providers consolidate and reengineer their care delivery and information-sharing processes to provide cost-effective integrated healthcare services across the continuum of care;
- payors reduce the cost of healthcare administration while providing financial incentives for medical providers to provide high-quality, cost-effective care;

- employers obtain healthy, productive, and informed employees at a reasonable cost;
- consumers take informed control of their health and work in partnership with physicians and payors to receive high-quality medical outcomes in the most appropriate clinical setting; and
- regulators ensure the system works through oversight, monitoring, and information dissemination.

Moving from the old healthcare model to the new healthcare model will not be easy. Because the entire healthcare industry is being dismantled and radically reconstructed, the structures, tools, and processes that worked and proved valuable in the old environment will not be successful in this new model. Instead, new approaches need to be developed to meet the significantly more complex and challenging operational requirements of the new healthcare model (i.e., information sharing and collection throughout the community and eventually the world). The Internet is ideal for this purpose, but only if its applications are designed to support organizational goals and implemented with sufficient technical architecture.

The Internet's potential to fulfill these needs is a primary motivation behind this book. CEOs, CIOs, and other healthcare executives are overwhelmed with hype about the Internet and intranets in trade journals and the national press. It is easy to think that the Internet is commodity-based and that its implementation is a "no brainer." However, this impression is dangerously far from the truth.

Although providing access is relatively simple, providing pertinent strategic applications is not. The Internet's value to healthcare providers lies in the contents that the applications offer. These contents must be highly customized and built around the needs of users with different backgrounds and different requirements. Well-designed and tested processes for developing content-based applications are still limited. Moreover, knowledgeable professionals with practical, hands-on Internet development experience are scarce and in high demand. The issues surrounding implementation are enormously complex, and executives need a solid foundation for understanding them.

Recognizing the need for knowledge of the Internet's practical uses, this book discusses the ramifications of the Internet as it relates to the business of healthcare and provides healthcare executives and managers with a business-oriented framework for understanding the current capabilities and limitations, the drivers of future change, and the potential business implications and applications of the Internet.

The book is divided into nine chapters designed to provide the logical building blocks necessary to understand the total picture of the Internet and its application to healthcare. The first two chapters provide general background on the Internet and explore new ways the Internet is being used to deliver innovative healthcare applications. Chapters 3 and 4 are completely new and look more deeply into two healthcare applications: physician integration and call centers. The final chapters discuss the future direction of the Internet and healthcare IT, examine healthcare processes and business strategies related to the Internet, and review security and other critically important issues.

One of the major challenges in writing this book is the rapid pace of change in the Internet arena. Whereas change in the computer industry was traditionally measured in annual cycles (much like the auto industry), an "Internet year" is now equivalent to three calendar months and is characterized not by incremental advancement but by monumental enhancement. Rather than focus on the technical details that change literally from moment to moment, this book intends to harness this energy by developing a business framework to understand the power and opportunity of the Internet.

Our goal is to help healthcare organizations understand and apply the power of the Internet by developing the information, processes, and organizations that will lead to better healthcare delivery.

Steve Ditto
Briggs Pille
Kent Gray
Maria Sundeen

1

The Internet Today

Aaron Garinger

How big is the Internet? Where is it heading? What do organizations need to know before they can position themselves for new advances, business opportunities, and threats? In all industries, CEOs, managers, and technologists are asking the questions that seem appropriate to structure the evolution of the Internet. Statistics highlighting the expansive growth of the Internet are still being released regularly. Volume, measured in numbers and types of users, is a closely monitored and often quoted statistic. Investments in advertising, web sites, intranets, and new business ventures also suggest an extensive commitment to entering this new market. With Internet web sites like *Physicians Online* (www.po.com/Welcome.html) boasting more than 170,000 registered physician users, healthcare appears to be enthusiastic about the Internet for the short term and to be positioning for usage over the long term.

Users

Cross-industry studies from numerous sources are attempting to measure and report the state of the Internet. Enough sources of Internet estimates and statistics exist that a web site has been established (www.CyberAtlas.com) to consolidate and report key information culled from these sources. Attempting to identify the Internet user population is not an exact process, because multiple studies use various methods and definitions. As shown in Table 1.1, estimates range from 40 to 62 million. If these are based on Internet addresses, the numbers of actual users may be higher.

The worldwide Internet user population in 1998 is estimated at 129.4 million. According to NUA, one of Europe's leading information consulting firms, the United States and Canada combined still have the largest percentage of Internet users (see Figure 1.1 for details). Although these numbers may appear trivial in terms of the worldwide population, they are significant when the total penetration of computing devices is considered. International Data Corp (IDC) predicts that the total number of Internet users will reach 163 million by 2000.

Although the numbers may reflect vast potential, it is interesting and useful to note the type of audience using these resources. The Georgia Institute of Technology's Graphic, Visualization, and Usability Center (GVU, www.cc.gatech.edu/gvu) conducts a survey every six months to examine detailed demographic profiles of Internet users, including gender, primary language, voter registration status, connection speed, frequency of use, and other items. As of the fall of 1997, 38 percent of Internet users were female, and nearly everyone in all age groups reported English as their primary language (90 to 96 percent). Most users were registered to vote (more than 83 percent), used the Internet on a daily basis

Table 1.1   Estimates of Internet Users as of 1997/1998

Source	Date	Definition	Users (in millions)
FIND/SVP (etrg.findsvp.com)	April 1997	Total U.S. adult users	40–45 million
Mediamark Research Inc. (MRI) (www.mediamark.com)	Spring 1997	Any cyber user in the U.S.	44.9 million
IntelliQuest (www.intelliquest.com)	February 1998	U.S. internet users	62 million (30.0% of total population)

Figure 1.1   Worldwide Internet User Population, as of 1998

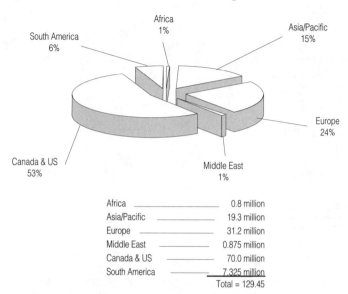

Africa		0.8 million
Asia/Pacific		19.3 million
Europe		31.2 million
Middle East		0.875 million
Canada & US		70.0 million
South America		7.325 million
		Total = 129.45

Source: www.nua.ie

(85 percent), and connected to the net at 33.6 kb modem speed. As far as occupation is concerned, Table 1.2 shows that healthcare providers composed about 2 percent of all male Internet users and 8 percent of all female net users.

Another measure of the increased usage of the Internet is the number of hours spent online. Other media, like television, have long measured consumer behavior in terms of the number of hours watched per week. According to a study by IntelliQuest, the average number of hours per week a user spends online jumped from 6.9 hours in 1996 to 9.8 hours in 1997.[1] This measurement is significant because the amount of time invested in exploring the Internet helps researchers gauge the amount and quality of available information of interest to users.

Consumers' comfort level is another factor that indicates the growth of Internet use. Research indicates that consumers are growing more and more comfortable with the prospect of performing everyday tasks online. For example, IntelliQuest reports that 60 percent of Internet users shop online, and that 17 percent feel comfortable enough to purchase online. The same study also notes

Table 1.2   Leading Occupations of Internet Users

	Male	*Female*
Business Professional/Accounting/Lawyer	15%	15%
Executive/Management	11	5
Engineering/Science	11	1
Technical/Programming	9	6
Skilled Trades	7	1
Sales	6	5
Government/Public Sector	6	3
Teacher	5	14
Retiree	5	3
Healthcare Provider	**2**	**8**
Clerical	—	6
Homemaker	—	13

Source: Find/SVP 1997.

that nearly half of all users attempt ten or more activities online (e.g., sending e-mail, accessing information, ordering a product) when they spend at least five hours a week on the Internet.[2]

As the quantity and quality of information available on the Internet increase, so does the value of the Internet to the user. For healthcare, Internet resources like specialty healthcare sites, healthcare-related newsgroups, specialty information delivery services, and other applications increase the value-per-hour spent online for the user. This value validates the healthcare industry's investment in the Internet.

Corporate Investment

The information supply-and-demand equation is constantly being calculated to determine investment potential. Corporate America, especially its healthcare segment, is embracing and investing in the Internet for multiple purposes. Some use the Internet to "push" products and services. Many organizations are now budgeting dollars to be spent on this medium as an advertising and marketing channel. However, the revenue of even the top volume Internet sites pales in comparison to traditional advertising channels like radio, TV, and print.

Still, investment in the form of new business ventures continues at a significant pace, in spite of some of the early and highly visible failures like the MCI cybermall. MCI has recently redirected efforts to become a dominant force in the international connectivity arena through its partnership with British Telecommunications. Overall, the global Internet market is expected to soar.

Investment in the development of a web presence or site is growing exponentially, and the cost of web sites is climbing as steadily as consumer interest. A recent survey by NetMarketing reports that the national median price of a simple web site rose from $25,000 in late 1997 to $44,500 in 1998. The median cost of marketing-oriented web sites has risen 78 percent since October 1997, and rates for medium-sized and larger marketers reported increases of 20 percent and 10 percent, respectively.[3]

Industry Development

Currently, a large portion of business and related revenues comes from the setup of the Internet through connectivity, servers, and Internet toolsets. Internet-related businesses are being created at an increasing rate. Electronic commerce in the form of financial transactions (e.g., home banking, online trading) and product purchasing (e.g., cybermalls, travel purchasing) are becoming more commonplace. Used medical equipment vendors have sprung up across the country, specializing in refurbished, unique, and high-cost equipment inventories. CME services are now available through the Internet (e.g., CMEWeb), as niche businesses find a place in the online world. In addition, publishing has taken on new forms with entries like Pointcast, a personalized information service; MSNBC, a joint venture between Microsoft and the television network; and C NET, a combination web site and cable-television channel.

Many industries are using the Internet to serve their business needs. Even by aggressive standards, the media and publishing industries are experiencing explosive growth in Internet deployment. Many magazine publications and newspapers like the *Wall Street Journal* are taking advantage of the low publishing cost, the low delivery cost, and the interactivity available through the Internet. With new forms of "microcharging," online magazines and newspapers can begin to charge the reader cents per article read. This charge will allow publishers to link the targeted value of the article received with its cost.

The financial sector is also looking to leverage the Internet to drive down transaction costs. Online sites like E*Trade Securities and Charles Schwab are showing that online trading can be convenient—5.3 million online-trading accounts have been opened to date. With commission structures declining, the Internet is poised to take up the trading channel opportunity.

Some estimates state that 90 percent of corporations are now evaluating intranet solutions for corporate Internet use. Intranet Productions International (IPI) reported that as of May 1997, the use of web servers for internal applications was growing at an annual rate of 40 percent worldwide and 60 percent in the United States.[4] Clearly, significant investment by businesses in intranets is expected to occur in the next few budget years.

Origin and History of the Internet

Although the growth statistics and corporate hopes for the Internet illustrate its vast potential for both businesses and consumers, the Internet was not designed for use in the business and technology arena. What is now known as the Internet was created for military and academic reasons rather than for business applications.

Many technologies have started as a result of government research and development funding focused on national security. Some of the core technologies in today's Internet started in the late 1960s in the Department of Defense (DOD). In 1969, a group within the DOD called the Advanced Research Projects Agency (ARPA) contracted with business, academic, and government researchers to collaborate on a computer network. This simple network was dubbed the ARPANET, and during the next decade, the network became a test bed for new communications technologies.

In 1972, the first e-mail message was successfully sent over the ARPANET, with an address that included the now ubiquitous @ symbol. By 1980, the ARPANET spanned the country and connected more than 400 host computers at universities, government locations, and military sites. Access to the network extended to more than 10,000 users, although the environment was still essentially the playground for scientists and other academics. In 1983, the ARPANET adopted a single method transmission control protocol/Internet protocol (TCP/IP) for computer systems communicating over the network. This standardization simplified the sending and receiving of data among incompatible computers and, in turn, spawned the creation of many new networks. In healthcare today, this characteristic standardization is creating opportunities among partners in a consolidating environment.

Another technology advancement emerged around 1984, when a domain-naming technology allowed a user-friendly name to be given as a means of reference to a computer. Today, many organizations and companies consider these domain names strategically important forms of representation (e.g., www.ibm.com, www.whitehouse.gov, and www.harvard.edu).

ARPANET provided the forum and set the foundation for the Internet as we know it today. At the turn of the decade, as ARPANET was being shut down, another network advancement was being made in Switzerland by Tim Berners-Lee at CERN, the European Laboratory for Particle Physics. This advancement, called the World Wide Web (WWW), allowed research documents of different formats to be converted to a standardized format that could be stored on centralized computers. CERN scientists could then create uniform documents and access them through a network, regardless of what computer they were using to access the documents or where those documents resided. Links to stored documents were called hypertext links; when selected, they would bring the requested document up on the computer screen. This greatly reduced the time needed to search for a particular document.

Marc Andreesen changed the face of the WWW in 1993 with the development of the first web browser, known as Mosaic. This breakthrough brought to the Internet the graphical view of information available to users through their personal computers. For the first time, users could use a mouse to point and click on desired information and access graphic displays on the screen across a wide variety of computer platforms.

The following years saw explosive growth in the number of network users and the expansion of the multiple physical networks composing the Internet. It is clear that the Internet is becoming entrenched as a common business tool, with a focus on attracting consumers to use the network. However, it is also clear that Internet development and widespread usage and acceptance have a long way to go. As the history of the Internet continues to be written, an effort is under way to increase the toolsets of the Internet and to make it more user-friendly.

Today's User-Friendly Internet Tools

One problem with the Internet is that in its current state, its consumer-friendly or user-friendly characteristics do not approach those of the common television or radio. Use of a television requires only a few straightforward commands, like on, off, and channel select. WebTV is attempting to bring the ease of access to the living room through the use of an inexpensive device that plugs into an ordinary television to enable web use.

In addition, several complementary products and technologies are helping to make the Internet more user-friendly. An example is a dynamic Microsoft information resource that searches and retrieves updates from the Internet for recent and relevant information. Another example is the increasing use of online graphical persons, known as avatars, to represent live individuals for online discussions. These sometimes cartoonish figures can depict speech and movement in a virtual, three-dimensional online world. The U.S. military is experimenting with the use of avatars for simulated battlefield triage and medical training. These avatars are simulations of infantry soldiers injured in battle with realistic injuries, vital signs, and lifelike characteristics. As more tools are made available and the Internet becomes more user-friendly, increasing numbers of consumers will be attracted to and feel comfortable in the online environment.

Where, then, will healthcare focus its efforts to adopt and leverage this technology? Reductions in administrative and transaction costs, increased enterprise access, increased physician communication, and remote and home diagnostics are just a few initial areas where Internet use can have a beneficial and definitive effect on business and patient care. As with any technology, applicability and fit must be measured before healthcare can realize the Internet's potential. When we achieve a balanced understanding of benefits, issues, and opportunities in a logical framework, we can accurately evaluate the effect that the Internet will have on the healthcare environment.

Notes

1. This study, published November 18, 1997, was found at www. intelliquest.com/press/release37.asp in September 1998. Current information about this area of interest is maintained at www. intelliquest.com.
2. This study was published February 5, 1998 and was found at www. intelliquest.com/press/release41.asp in September 1998.
3. This survey was found in the NetMarketing archives at www.netb2b. com/cgi-bin/cgi_wpi_archive/wpi/98/06/01/article.2 in September 1998.
4. This information was found at www.ipip.com/intranet/ipstat01.htm in September 1998.

2

The Role of the Internet in Healthcare: Opportunities

Tim Webb

$\mathbf{T}$he opportunities for Internet use in health-care are just beginning to be explored. The Internet is still growing and changing, and its progress and developments are not easily charted. The pivotal point for much of this technological development lies in some futuristic gray space, where clinical, financial, and consumer information can be easily stored, analyzed, retrieved, and shared among consumers, patients, clinicians, healthcare delivery systems, health plans, and insurers. As the Internet grows, these opportunities will be explored, tested, and fulfilled.

For the healthcare industry to take advantage of the opportunities afforded by the Internet, several other changes must occur. First, the process of delivering healthcare, wellness, and education must change. Once these changes have been implemented, they can be supported by academic research, competition in the marketplace, and real-world IDSs responding to those competitive pressures.

This chapter, which presents a futuristic vision of healthcare, will suggest a central role for the Internet and discuss its potential effect on the process of healthcare delivery. Included in the discussion will be examples of applications from leading institutions currently using the Internet or Internet tools. Opportunities for future applications will also be explored.

Future Scenario

John Smith is 65 years old and retired, and he has a history of heart trouble. He spends most of his time at home or traveling around the country to visit friends. Around his wrist he wears a bracelet that is connected by wireless cellular communications to the Internet. It continuously sends his electrocardiogram (EKG) to his physician's computer system through the Internet. If an abnormality is identified, the physician's computer system automatically alerts his doctor.

One day, while John is taking his afternoon walk, his bracelet detects abnormal heart rhythms. John has not yet experienced any discomfort. His bracelet transmits the abnormal EKG information to his physician, who is paged. The physician's computer system generates a message, which is transmitted via the Internet, to summon an ambulance. John's bracelet also includes a global positioning system (GPS) receiver. This device sends his exact position to his physician and the paramedics—all through the Internet.

The ambulance arrives at John's location within five minutes of the initial abnormal EKG reading. At the same time, the physician in the emergency room (ER) is reviewing John's EKG in near-real time. While John is in transit, the ER physician gives instructions to the paramedics. Because the physician has clinical information captured at the time of the occurrence and access to John's history through a health information network (HIN), the physician is able to make an accurate diagnosis and apply an appropriate and cost-effective form of treatment.

The results and implications of this scenario are many. First, John's life is potentially saved because of the early detection of a life-threatening medical condition. Time is saved by the automatic notification of John's physician, who is able to make an informed decision on the basis of access to real-time clinical information. The ER physician is also able to make an informed decision about John's care based on access to continuous, real-time EKG information and patient history. Finally, costs are reduced by avoiding unnecessary tests and the possible expense of an overnight stay in the hospital.

The Case for Changed Processes

The primary objectives of many technology implementations are to improve clinical decision making, reduce administrative costs, and improve competitive position by focusing on convenient access to care. Technology will play a key role in integrating information across numerous sources, making it meaningful for the patient, provider, insurer, and public sector. Can technology itself effect these changes, or does the process of care delivery need to change as well?

Technology will never replace the patient relationship with the physician or provider. However, the current process of delivering care, which was built around paper medical records, must be updated to take advantage of the technology available today. Updating the business and clinical processes is a top priority for researchers and IDSs. Researchers at leading institutions like Beth Israel Hospital in New York are identifying opportunities to improve outcomes through the use of standardized care protocols and integrated information systems. In addition, incorporating information technology into clinical processes is a top priority for IDSs. As future visions and scenarios for the use of technology are presented, keep in mind that the existing processes may need to change to take advantage of Internet technologies.

Are Changed Processes Required to Take Advantage of Internet Technologies?

A series of articles in the *New England Journal of Medicine*[1] concluded that healthcare quality can only be achieved by capturing detailed clinical data, measuring the quality of care, focusing on the process of delivering care, and focusing on the continuum of care. Capturing clinical data requires real-time communications, changes in the processes of care, and an integrated information system to achieve this communication and change.

The Internet can accomplish two vital tasks: the integration of information across disparate platforms and large geographic areas, and the support of the development of clinical decision support systems. The Internet also affects the administrative cost of delivering care by automating or changing inefficient processes like scheduling a visit to a primary care physician. Finally, the greatest potential—and challenge—of the Internet lies in its ability to support customer-focused delivery of services (see Figure 2.1).

These changed processes will start with a managed care organization responsible for maintaining health. They will be predicated on continuing relationships with primary care physicians and any and all necessary specialists. Tables 2.1, 2.2, and 2.3 display examples of ways that current institutions are using the Internet to support clinical, administrative, and financial applications.

Table 2.1 shows some of the clinical applications that may be enhanced using the Internet. Much research has been done and much progress has been made in the area of clinical decision making. Researchers for the department of medical informatics at Columbia University in New York have been using the Internet to rapidly develop clinical applications. Key components of their system are an integrated patient database and a common vocabulary for translating medical information between different clinical systems. One example of integrated functional-

Figure 2.1   Processes for the 21st Century Integrated Delivery Network

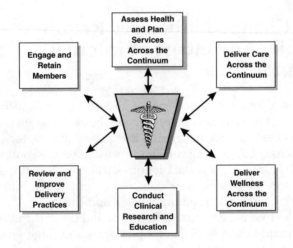

ity is the ability of the physician to initiate a MEDLINE search (www.cpmc.columbia.edu/cisdemo) (when viewing a lab result).

Clinical results reporting is very important because it helps physicians make timely decisions about care. Sentara Health System in Norfolk, Virginia, an integrated delivery network, provides results from hospitals and laboratories to physicians in real time via their in-house developed web-based application called SPIN (Sentara Physicians Integrated Network). SPIN can deliver results via web application, e-mail, or facsimile.

Fletcher Allen Healthcare in Vermont is embarking on a $30 million investment in telemedicine. The network links healthcare providers from around the state into a single, universal network. The clinical benefits of this network should save patients and

Table 2.1   Potential Enhancements of Clinical Applications Using the Internet

Healthcare Applications	*Benefits*	*Potential Issues*
Clinical Decision Making	• Improved quality of outcomes • Reduced cost through adherence to standard protocols	• Technical barriers to developing virtual data warehouses • Time required to develop
Clinical Results Reporting	• Ease of distribution • Ease of reference	• Timeliness of data • Patient confidentiality • Application interfaces
Consultation	• Improved patient care	• State licensing • Patient confidentiality
Telemedicine	• Patient cost reduction for designated services • Improved access to clinics	• Cost effectiveness • Quality of service
Conferencing	• Standardized document transfer • Standardized video conferencing	• Quality of images/video • Limited access to equipment • Bandwidth limitations

Table 2.2   Potential Enhancements of Administrative
            Applications Using the Internet

Healthcare Applications	Benefits	Potential Issues
CME	• Expanded staff participation • Ongoing certification • Collaborative studies	• User acceptance of computer-based learning techniques
Scheduling	• Enterprise scheduling for department/staff and location resources • Integrated patient demographics and payor information	• Patient confidentiality • Schedule management
Marketing/Advertisement	• Business-to-business marketing • Patient-oriented marketing • Community-based participation • Surveys/studies	• Currently limited access to audience • Limited control of audience response
Messaging	• Business-to-business connectivity (EDI) • Business-to-patient communication • Patient-to-business communication	• Latency • Quality of service
Transcription	• Remote access	• Patient confidentiality

physicians millions of dollars in lost productivity traveling from location to location for consultations. In addition, the network will support standard video conferencing.

Because advances in healthcare delivery are happening as quickly as those in technology, physicians are challenged to keep updating their knowledge of clinical practices and disease management protocols. CME, already a major use of the Internet, helps fulfill this need. For example, there is an interactive patient

Table 2.3   Potential Enhancements of Financial Applications
                Using the Internet

Healthcare Applications	Benefits	Potential Issues
Payment/ Billing	• Simplified EDI for patient billing • Payment status	• Connection reliability • Authentication • Verification

Research	• Standardized access to:
	  – Academic information
	  – Provider information
	  – Payor information
		• Plagiarism
		• Content verification

simulation in which patient cases are presented and the user can interact with questions (www.uchsc.edu). One of the best Internet sites on the topic of online education and research is CliniWeb, provided by the Oregon Health Sciences University. CliniWeb contains 2,500 uniform resource locators (URLs) for clinical content indexed by disease (www.ohsu.edu/cliniweb/).

Messaging, or e-mail, is quickly becoming a commonplace communication service, so commonplace that many professionals include their e-mail addresses on their business cards. Professors and students often use e-mail to schedule office appointments and communicate about assignments. Organizations have also instituted internal e-mail systems so employees can communicate with one another without generating stacks of memos or phone interruptions.

E-mail has not yet become a standard part of the provider-patient relationship, but this area is ripe for fundamental process changes. Appointments can be scheduled and rescheduled using e-mail communication, which would free the nurse or assistant from answering phone calls and eliminate the patient frustration associated with being put on hold for long periods of time. Physicians are only now beginning to use e-mail extensively. An example is Northwestern Memorial Hospital in Chicago, which implemented e-mail across the management and physician staff several years ago. Their system now handles more than 40,000 e-mail messages per month.

Benefits

The benefits of Internet technology are realized by the patient as well as the physician, integrated delivery network, and managed care organization. The benefits include improved satisfaction on the part of the patient, cost reduction, improved quality, and enhanced competitive position. Using the Internet, patients will have greater access to their physicians. The patient/physician relationship that results will be dependent, at least in part, on the quality and reliability of the information transported over the Internet link.

Another potential benefit is the ability to minimize cost through education. As patients become more responsible for their own health, they exert control over the cost of healthcare. When provided with research information, standard care protocols, and timely access to their physicians, patients may be better able to control costs from the beginning of care. The Internet provides patients with a resource to access information relevant to their health situation. This potential to educate themselves empowers patients to become aware of their symptoms early, possibly resulting in lower acuity levels before starting formal treatment. Additional cost reduction may come from early detection and treatment. Through timely and frequent communications with their patients over the Internet, care providers will have better information with which to make early diagnoses, which have been shown in many cases to result in more successful treatment and recovery.

Additional benefits may result from the time savings the Internet provides. Online appointment scheduling will allow people to accomplish this task quickly and efficiently. If patients are able to schedule appointments after work hours, the effect on their productivity during business hours (e.g., waiting on hold to talk to the physician's office) may be reduced (see Figure 2.2).

The Internet may also enhance the quality and enable the standardization of care across wide geographic areas. With access to the latest clinical trials and research findings, primary care physicians in the smallest rural environment can be as well informed as specialists in large cities.

Figure 2.2   How Information Technology Strategy Affects
Relative Productivity

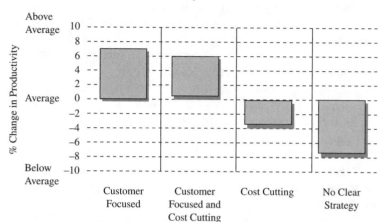

Market Forces

Where healthcare and Internet technology converge, there will be many opportunities to expand and enhance access to information. Although we believe that many of the applications we have discussed will come to fruition, diverse market forces will shape and tailor the Internet, customizing its development and use in healthcare. Four primary areas in healthcare hold opportunities for these market forces:

1. competitive opportunities;
2. patient opportunities;
3. provider opportunities; and
4. insurer/plan opportunities.

The following sections examine in detail the opportunities likely to be exploited by these market forces, the benefits the Internet provides each group, and the areas in which Internet use is likely to expand.

Competitive Opportunities

Just as the banking industry is looking to the Internet to radically change the way it provides customer service, leading healthcare organizations are attempting to use the Internet to change their relationships with patients and health plan members, tapping into the opportunity that this technology is offering.

As we all know, competition in the healthcare industry is increasing. HMOs are competing with traditional insurers, integrated delivery networks are competing with stand-alone hospitals, and not-for-profits are competing with for-profit hospital chains. Although competition is relatively new to healthcare, there are well-established guidelines within other industries on ways to use information technology to be proactive in the marketplace.

Easy and reliable access to services advances competitiveness and enhances productivity. A survey of all industries by *Information Week* concluded that organizations can be more productive if they have a customer-focused strategy and apply technology to that business strategy in a focused manner[2]: "What matters to customers is the quality, cost, timeliness, and appropriateness for a company's products and services."[3] Healthcare organizations that use the Internet in patient-focused and physician-focused strategies are more likely to benefit from enhanced relationships and improved processes (see Figure 2.3).

In the 1990s, with two-career families and numerous after-school and after-work activities, convenient access can be considered a marketing "jewel." The popularity of catalog buying and the Home Shopping Channel suggests a significant market for this convenience. The Internet provides convenient access similar to the telephone and television in terms of its ability to reach millions of people and convey vast amounts of information.

Healthcare already has several progressive Internet users in the public domain. Patients can find such insurers as Blue Cross and Blue Shield of Massachusetts and such health systems as Columbia/HCA using the Internet for marketing and educational purposes. With this infrastructure in place, these organizations are laying the foundation for future interactive applications like appointment scheduling from home.

Figure 2.3   Opportunities for the Internet in Healthcare

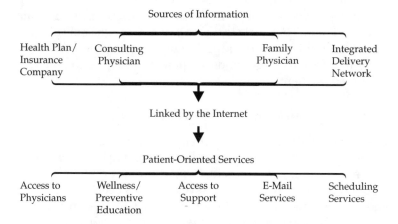

Sources of Information

| Health Plan/ Insurance Company | Consulting Physician | Family Physician | Integrated Delivery Network |

Linked by the Internet

Patient-Oriented Services

| Access to Physicians | Wellness/ Preventive Education | Access to Support | E-Mail Services | Scheduling Services |

Future scenario

> After putting the kids to bed, Dan finally has time to think about things that didn't get done during his long day at work. He sits down at his PC and, through the Internet, logs into his primary care physician's web site. After entering the appropriate passwords, he is able to see available times when he could schedule an appointment. He enters some text regarding the nature of his visit, being as specific as he wants. A few more clicks, and he is done.

Certainly, vendors will have continued interest in developing applications for the Internet. Recent estimates put average investment by organizations at 3 to 9 percent of their total information system (IS) budgets for Internet/intranet technology. The focus for organizations' future investment in Internet technology should be high-impact, high-return applications.

Opportunities for the Patient

From a patient's perspective, the Internet can provide high-value and high-impact functionality to preventive care. Health education, if convenient, relevant, and encouraged, can improve the opportunities for early detection and diagnosis of many ailments.

Convenient access to information, enabled by Internet technologies, can enhance the care process; specifically, Internet technologies can provide access to information that can help alleviate chronic ailments like diabetes or asthma. Although some of these patient care and educational applications are available today, most are still in various stages of development, including the Internet access requirements.

Preventive healthcare and education

Preventive healthcare is the objective of most managed care organizations, the result being improved wellness and reduced long-term cost. As Benjamin Franklin said, "an ounce of prevention is worth a pound of cure." In the past, however, it has been very difficult and expensive for managed care organizations to communicate targeted marketing and wellness-related information regularly to members. Direct mail is antiquated because of its one-way nature. The Internet provides an interactive medium for announcing wellness screenings to a select audience in a timely, proactive manner. Consider the implications of allowing participants to register online without requiring a telephone call or someone to answer that call.

Access to care

Imagine the number of people, every day, looking for a new primary care physician or specialist. Several organizations have established sophisticated physician-referral programs that match the patient's desire for location, office hours, experience, education, years in practice, and so on. Typically, these services are provided only during business hours. On the Internet, however, this application can be provided 24 hours a day, seven days a week. Once the potential patient has narrowed down a selection of physicians, details like the physician's credentials and experience can be reviewed at home. Columbia/HCA is offering this function today on its web server.

Once a physician has been selected, a patient can then schedule an appointment. Through hot links or an embedded application, the patient should be able to go directly to the physician's schedule. Specific open times would be shown graphically and, through a simple query, the patient should be able to find and schedule a convenient time. In addition, a map or directions to the office can be provided.

In this scenario, the patient would enter the purpose for the visit. If the patient has not seen the physician before, other information may be required; the patient may be asked to complete a basic history and physical to provide the physician with relevant data. The patient may also be asked to provide the names of past physicians so they may be contacted via e-mail for the relevant medical history.

If the patient cannot find a convenient time or needs to speak with the physician's office, an e-mail message may be generated and sent to the physician's administrative staff. In the future, a voice conversation may also be integrated within the same Internet access session.

Care delivery

Once a patient has seen the doctor and has started on a course of treatment, regular communication with his or her physician is important. E-mail is a convenient, time-insensitive method allowing doctor and patient to stay in constant communication.

During the course of treatment, the physician will want to share results of diagnostic tests with the patient. These results may be e-mailed by the testing lab to the physician, who can then forward them to the patient with an interpretation and changes to the treatment plan. When the physician wants the patient to become more knowledgeable about his or her condition, this education can be provided through the Internet, again at the patient's convenience.

Managing financial and quality aspects

During the course of treatment, the financial and quality aspects of the patient's care will need to be addressed. Even with managed care, the patient will need to have contact with the insurance company. These communications may be initiated by the insurance company to monitor the treatment; however, they may also include questionnaires regarding the quality of care provided by the physician and other providers. The patient may also have the need to initiate communications with the insurance company regarding second opinions, the costs of alternative treatment plans, and so on.

Patients should expect their local care providers to use the Internet to provide convenient access to information and services seven days a week, 24 hours a day. Based on the ever-increasing number of home PCs, many patients may prefer to send their family physician an e-mail to discuss healthcare concerns. Just as important, access to services (e.g., scheduling an appointment or diagnostic tests) will provide real value to the patients who prefer this type of interaction.

Opportunities for the Provider and Clinician

The people focused on the care delivery process have many demands placed on them and little time for extraneous activities. The Internet provides many opportunities to save providers, physicians, nurses, and other clinicians time and money. The Internet was developed as a teaching and research tool for sharing information and is still well suited to this task; however, it also offers a new medium to support the physician-patient relationship, which has suffered in recent years because of physicians' piles of paperwork. If deployed properly, convenient access to clinical-patient information, specialists, and managed care companies should save time for the physician and provide the caregiver with more complete and more timely information.

Physician education

Healthcare delivery is changing at a rapid pace, in large part as a result of extensive clinical research. The information from formal research studies and clinical trials for new drugs improves the understanding of disease prevention and treatment. Physicians need to have access to the latest academic research to keep abreast of diagnosis and treatment trends and breakthroughs, and the Internet can play a vital role by enabling physicians to retrieve this information quickly and conveniently.

Professional development and CME are also important issues for physicians. Today, in Internet "chat rooms," physicians can communicate and share experiences without extensive travel or a decrease in productivity. In the not-too-distant future, through interactive learning on the Internet, physicians may be able to receive specialized training and certification in knowledge-based treatments and procedures.

The Internet can bridge the information gap by allowing physicians to share information about specific patients, treatment plans, and history in a cost-effective and efficient manner. With the convenience of access to the Internet, physicians will be able to better manage their time while providing improved care to patients. In addition, as physicians are developing treatment plans for their patients, online access to disease-specific research can enhance their ability to provide patients with the latest information.

Care delivery and management

Because physicians are looking for ways to save time and money while still providing quality care, tools such as the Internet will be in high demand. The Internet can provide such invaluable resources as timely information about new drugs, access to treatment protocols, and even convenient access to colleagues to discuss challenging cases or patient-specific consultations.

The delivery of episodic treatment begins when a patient first communicates with a healthcare provider. Today, this communication may take place by means of a telephone call to a nurse on call with an insurance company, or through an initial office visit with the physician. Care delivery tends to be a reactive process, and traditionally, the caregiver's reaction was limited to office hours or an answering service for emergency situations. The Internet provides a more effective means of communicating with the patient than current methods do. E-mail can be more efficient than other forms of communication, because it enables the physician to respond to messages at the end of the day or at a convenient time and place without making numerous telephone calls.

During the treatment process, physicians may need to confer with or refer a patient to a specialist. These referrals commonly represent a huge gap in the continuum of patient care because of the physician's inability to share or send patient information. This inability is frequently the result of a lack of enabling technology. As busy as most physicians are, returning telephone calls to patients is an inefficient use of their time. An e-mail message will allow physicians to refer patients to specialists quickly, efficiently, and conveniently. The technology would also allow a physician to copy a patient on e-mail referrals easily. The Internet can also provide a medium to attach low bandwidth monitors, such as neonatal, cardiac, or diabetes monitors, to a patient through a PC and to transmit this information in a timely manner to the necessary institution or doctor.

Managing provider relationships

Communication with insurance companies will continue to be a requirement for care providers well into the future. These communications may address routine treatment protocols, case management, referrals, and financial aspects of the care plan. Although physicians may never appreciate being monitored and "second-guessed," the timeliness of Internet communications can prevent misunderstandings and can result in near real-time resolution of issues. With the current process, issues may not be identified until some time after care has been delivered.

Opportunities for Health Plans/Insurers: The Managed Care Environment

Managed care organizations focus on managing the quality and cost of healthcare delivery. In managed care, there is growing emphasis on wellness and demand management as possible approaches to managing quality and cost. Providing information to consumers, particularly to patients with chronic ailments, will help lessen healthcare usage.

In the future, it will be relatively common for consumers to establish a voice conversation with a customer service representative while linked to a web site over a dial-up connection. However, this future will depend more on advances in the public telephone network than on the ability of an IDS to go online.

Physician linkage is another area for competitive structuring. Intranet functions will likely be provided to physicians through integrated delivery networks that offer access to complete clinical information and support for managing capitated contracts. However, many application systems currently use proprietary communications and interfaces, which limit access to these systems. Today, the best use of the Internet for insurers or managed care plans is as a marketing tool. The Internet has become world-renowned for its ability to overcome time and distance barriers between people and information.

Wellness and education

For managed care companies to be successful financially, they need to aggressively encourage their members to practice healthy lifestyles. They therefore need to use enabling technology to communicate effectively with plan members and monitor member compliance with wellness activities. The Internet provides an inexpensive tool to target the distribution of information (e.g., immunization reminders, annual checkups) to specific plan members. Most health plans have a difficult time communicating with members once they are part of a plan, a problem that is largely attributable to limited systems access and the cost and ineffectiveness of direct-mail marketing campaigns.

One Internet activity that has won popularity with users and customers is the healthcare chat group, which focuses on people with similar health issues (e.g., high blood pressure). Patients can share information with one another, provide and receive emotional support, share experiences, ask questions, and obtain advice. The groups offer "the potential for online networking to provide new health benefits, improve communication, and encourage collaboration beyond traditional healthcare models."[4] They can reduce the feeling of isolation many patients have. Because patients are often uncomfortable with face-to-face communication, they may not attend support groups offered in person; "[a]ttending an [online] support group is less intimidating than attending a face-to-face group, and it is also more convenient."[5]

Access to care

Once patients believe they need professional healthcare, they may initiate a call to a triage nurse employed by the health plan. The opportunity exists for the Internet to provide an additional, convenient method of accessing a nurse or physician to ask questions about a specific medical condition. The follow-up from the initial contact may be a telephone call or e-mail with specific instructions (e.g., see your primary care provider). The managed care organization can then implement "demand management" by directing the patient to the most cost-effective form of treatment, a capability that has tremendous benefits for all concerned.

Once a patient is in a treatment plan, the managed care organization may use the Internet to refer that patient to a specialist.

This referral management process is normally a paper-driven and time-consuming process. With the Internet, however, the process can be streamlined considerably, reducing the cost.

Patient support groups

During treatment, ongoing communications and information exchanges with the patient and their families may provide valuable support. For example, the Internet is currently being used as a virtual support group for families of at-home Alzheimer's patients. Clearly, one of the benefits of the Internet is its ability to provide real-time communications without transporting patients, thereby minimizing the need to transport patients to face-to-face meetings and office visits, as well as the associated expenses.

Problems and Issues

Because of healthcare's increasing dependency on information and technology, applications and information will have to be managed and updated regularly. Many healthcare Internet sites have been developed with static content. Patients may visit a web site once or twice, but they will not continue to come back if the content is not regularly updated and enhanced. In healthcare, informational demands are too dynamic not to have frequently updated content. Other issues for web sites include financing, access, security or privacy, performance, access to "good" information, and technical breakdowns.

Because healthcare will essentially become more commercial, it is probably a natural transition for pharmaceutical companies to begin major sponsorship of web sites with specific health systems (e.g., Columbia/HCA's site www.columbia-hca.com) to gain market recognition. The benefits of commercialization include the ability to support programs that are difficult to fund otherwise—for example, corporate-sponsored, health-related activities (e.g., "fun walks") and scholarships.

It is also important to note that the lower-income patients still have limited access to home computers; therefore, these initiatives will not reach many people, at least not in the near future. Therefore, a secondary system must be established to assist certain elements of the population. Efforts are under way in communities to provide computers and Internet access, via kiosks, in libraries, shopping malls, and so on. Until PCs are in virtually every home, universal Internet access will be impossible; therefore, multiple approaches to providing patient access to information or clinical resources will have to be supported.

Security will continue to be one of the most sensitive issues restricting use of the Internet. The Internet is still a loose affiliation of systems and networks with very little central control, and security is left to the end user. Even the CIA has had its web server infiltrated! Fortunately, technical developments to support the electronic transfer of money over the Internet will be transportable to healthcare. In addition, many organizations are developing tightly controlled intranets with proprietary networks to support their most sensitive applications and data.

As increasing amounts of graphics and images are transported from web sites to end users, cost and performance affect implementation and response time and may act as barriers to physician or patient usage. Considering competition among telephone companies and recent legislation encouraging that competition, higher-bandwidth circuits are expected to be available to home and small-business users at the same or slightly higher cost as dial-up services today. In addition, the advent of WebTV could bring the Internet into many more homes affordably. In the meantime, developers of web-based and Internet-based services should be conscious of the need to keep their services simple to provide high performance to their users.

Many physicians are concerned about their patients having access to too much information, some of which may not be from the best sources. The information content of web sites is not now and probably will not in the future be monitored for accuracy. One solution is for physicians to point their patients, using "hot-links," from their web site toward sites with factual, validated research and educational information.

Finally, like any other network service, the Internet is subject to technical breakdowns. Service providers like America Online (AOL) provide access to the Internet for millions of users. AOL has had more than its share of technical difficulties, mostly related to growth. If we expect physicians to become reliant on the Internet, there must be a reliable network supporting access seven days a week, 24 hours a day. Users who expect this type of performance will help create and drive competitive pressure on Internet service providers (ISPs) to enhance the fault tolerance capabilities of their networks.

Conclusion

By the time this book is released, there will surely be many more Internet healthcare sites available than at the time of writing. Although many health-related organizations currently employ Internet technology and use Internet access and sites, only a handful are truly optimizing the potential of the information superhighway. Columbia/HCA has been mentioned several times in this chapter, for good reason. Columbia views information technology as a competitive tool and invests in it aggressively.

Because of technology limitations, some of the most innovative and effective applications will not be developed or implemented for months or years into the future. However, here are some examples of future applications that may be Internet-enabled:

- All significant patient information captured and stored electronically
- Wireless access to the Internet required to support the capabilities
- High-speed digital service at affordable costs to bring the Internet into the home
- Support for simultaneous voice, data, and video across the Internet.

Notes

1. "Quality in Healthcare," a six-part series in the *New England Journal of Medicine* in 1996: Blumenthal, D. 1996. "Quality of Care: What Is It?" *New England Journal of Medicine* 335 (12): 891–94; Brook, R. H., E. A. McGlynn, and P. D. Cleary. 1996. "Measuring Quality of Care." *New England Journal of Medicine* 335 (13): 996–70; Chassin, M. R. 1996. "Improving the Quality of Care." *New England Journal of Medicine* 335

(14): 1060–63; Blumenthal, D. 1996. "The Origins of the Quality of Care Debate." *New England Journal of Medicine* 335 (15): 1146–49; Berwick, D. M. 1996. "Payment by Capitation and the Quality of Care Debate." *New England Journal of Medicine* 335 (16): 1146–49; Blumenthal, D., and A. M. Epstein. 1996. "The Role of Physicians in the Future of Quality Management." *New England Journal of Medicine* 335 (17): 1328–31.

2. Brynjolfsson, E., and L. Hitt. 1996. "The Customer Counts." *Information Week* 596 (September 9). www.InfoWeek.com.

3. Violino, B. 1996. "The Biggest and the Best." *Information Week* 596 (September 9): 48. www.InfoWeek.com.

4. Scolamiero, S. 1997. "Support Groups in Cyberspace." *MD Computing* 14 (1).

5. Scolamiero, S. 1997. "Support Groups in Cyberspace." *MD Computing* 14 (1).

3

Implications of the Internet: The Physician's Perspective

Peter M. Kilbridge, M.D., and
Michael Schneider, M.D.

T he emergence of the Internet has had an enormous effect on the healthcare industry, and the remainder of this book examines ways in which healthcare organizations can make use of this technology to advance their business goals. Perhaps less clear, however, is the effect the Internet has had on the daily routine of one particularly important category of end user: the practicing physician. In this chapter, we discuss the implications of the Internet for physicians, today and in the near future.

Physicians encounter numerous information-management needs on daily, hourly, and even minute-to-minute bases. These needs include access to patient-specific clinical data (e.g., lab results, dictated summaries), access to payor information regarding benefits and authorization, access to claims submissions to payors, communication with colleagues and patients, and access to current medical literature. Eventually, the Internet will affect all of these needs in some way; in many respects, it is already doing so.

The Internet has introduced a new complexity into the physician-patient relationship in several ways. The Internet makes vast amounts of information on health and medicine easily available to the public; this information previously would have required cumbersome legwork and many hours of research to locate. The Internet also has introduced new forums of communication: disease-specific interest groups and bulletin boards have proliferated, and the widespread availability of e-mail has lowered barriers to communication among patients and between patients and providers. Practicing physicians must develop a basic understanding for themselves of the ways to use the Internet, to comprehend the variety of resources available to them and their patients.

Access to Patient Care Data

Practicing physicians require rapid access to many types of clinical information, such as the results of laboratory tests (from chemistry or hematology) or transcribed reports (e.g., pathology, radiology, nuclear medicine reports, consultation notes, or hospital discharge summaries). Outpatient clinics, commercial laboratories, diagnostic centers, or hospitals may generate these reports. Such information is delivered to physicians by a variety of routes. Offices adjacent to a hospital campus may have direct access to inpatient results reporting systems; alternatively, physicians may be able to access a hospital's computer system by modem from remote sites. However, it remains common for physicians to receive reports from laboratories and hospitals by fax, courier, or mail.

Hospitals and integrated delivery networks increasingly rely on Internet-based technologies—intranets—to provide physicians with access to hospital data over internal, secure networks. Such access deploys Internet browser technology to provide a common user interface, allowing users to view results from disparate hospital or delivery network information systems. This approach allows physicians to access the hospital network without investing in specialized hardware and software (other than a browser-equipped desktop computer), thereby offering the ease of access of the Internet within a secure network environment. Some of the early examples of this type of system include the University of Minnesota web CIS,[1] the Columbia-Presbyterian WWW CIS,[2] and the Artemis project in West Virginia.[3] The CareWeb project, implemented at CareGroup in Boston following the merger of two hospitals, grants emergency department physicians access to patient information from multiple legacy databases and facilitates the consolidation of emergency care in a single location.[4]

Some organizations are experimenting with granting physicians secure access to their internal systems remotely by means of the Internet, thereby permitting access from any location. Security issues constitute the overwhelming obstacle to broad adoption of this model. Although this issue has not been resolved entirely, it seems likely that technical advances will render security significantly less problematic in the future. Current Health Care Financing Administration (HCFA) restrictions regarding Internet transmission of patient-identifiable information will become more manageable as new standards are adopted.[5] As security measures improve and acceptance of the technology becomes more widespread, the demand for this form of access will increase.

In addition to offering intranet access to patient results, hospitals and integrated delivery networks are making such resources as institutional clinical guidelines, provider directories, legacy system clinical data,[6] and literature search engines available online. These are frequently made available from the institution's Internet or intranet home page. Access to a standard institutional e-mail system is a particularly valuable feature, offered by some organizations at little or no cost to physicians. E-mail is the Internet function most frequently used by physicians, both for conducting administrative communication and, increasingly, for corresponding with patients (this use is discussed later in this chapter). Some organizations offer Internet access to their affiliated physicians, acting as their Internet service provider.

Disease management—the management of patients with chronic illnesses across the continuum of care, including in the home—is another area where the Internet is playing an increasingly important role. Many health plans and disease management companies are looking to Internet technology, in concert with sophisticated telephone applications, to establish connectivity with patients in their homes and other settings.[7] Medical devices designed for use by the patient in the home may facilitate the gathering of important monitoring data; in the future, such devices could conceivably be configured to transmit their data directly over the Internet. This would permit transmission of such quantitative physiologic data as vital signs, cardiogram tracings, and oxygen saturation, as well as text messages (e.g., medication reminders, questions about medications, new complaints) from the patient directly to the care manager and physician. Used in this way, the Internet will allow physicians and case managers to track the progress of their patients more closely than has been possible in the past, permitting them to intervene earlier if the patient's condition begins to deteriorate.[8]

The Internet and related technologies loosely categorized as "telemedicine" are affecting the delivery of care over distances in several important ways. Certain medical specialties—particularly those that make heavy use of imaging—can now be practiced in sites remote from the point of patient care, as high resolution images can be transmitted over the Internet using new digital imaging technologies. Teleradiology is the most common example; radiographs can be interpreted by a radiologist many miles from the patient's location, and consultations among specialists can be performed over great distances.[9] Although issues of reimbursement and licensure for distance medicine have slowed the deployment of these technologies, there seems little doubt that they will continue to change the way in which medicine is practiced, particularly in rural areas.[10]

Access to Payor Data

Health plans have turned to the Internet to share plan information with providers in an attempt to improve operational efficiencies and thus lower costs, as well as to improve customer satisfaction. Several health plans have placed product benefit and authorization information on an Internet web site to facilitate the processes of referral authorization and eligibility checking. Providers can review member eligibility, plan details, plan formularies, and care guidelines. Some plans offer electronic data interchange (EDI) for claims submission over encrypted Internet links.

One health plan has incorporated a sophisticated, intranet-linked referral management system into its call center function.[11] The system enables direct referral to a specialist by triage nurses according to complaint-specific protocols. Built-in managed care eligibility guidelines ensure referral within authorized physician networks, except in the case of an emergency. Thus, the system performs a combination of referral management based on medical necessity and referral authorization. The interface between the core clinical system and the call center is a key feature of the system; it allows triage nurses to view patient clinical data at the time of the call.

Another payor has adopted Internet technology to facilitate the referral authorization process.[12] Its primary motivation was to reduce administrative costs by improving the efficiency of communications between providers and payors.

Access to Medical Knowledge

Physicians regularly refer to all manner of medical literature, and the Internet has made this task considerably more convenient. All of the major medical literature search engines are accessible by means of web-based interfaces. Other information sources have sprung up solely because of the advantages of delivering content over the Internet. The National Library of Medicine (NLM) offers its Medline database free to Internet users by means of Grateful Med and PubMed. In addition, the government has made a concerted effort to offer access to its professional medical content through a customizable search engine (www.healthfinder.org/justforyou/hlthprofs.htm) and through web sites sponsored by the Agency for Health Care Policy and Research (AHCPR), the National Institutes of Health (NIH), the NLM, and the Department of Health and Human Services. Some provider organizations have made electronic, full-text versions of the major medical textbooks accessible over their intranets. All of the major medical journals have web pages where users can view the tables of contents, selected articles, and abstracts from current and past issues. Many have all of their articles available to subscribers online.

The sharing of expert advice among colleagues has been facilitated by the Internet. Electronic mail is the most commonly used application among physicians, and many provider organizations offer e-mail access to affiliated physicians at little or no cost. Although physicians' use of e-mail remains primarily administrative, the medium is being used with increasing frequency for consultations, arranging referrals, and other patient care-related tasks. Listservers (e-mail-based discussion lists) are popular for peer-to-peer interactions and often include practitioners from around the globe.[13] Distance learning programs using Internet and telemedicine technology are becoming increasingly common, offering continuing medical education and remote access to grand rounds at teaching hospitals. In a survey of anesthesiologists, 81 percent stated they had changed their practice based on information they had obtained using the Internet.[14]

All manner of bulletin boards and chat rooms have appeared, catering to generalists and specialists alike. Of course, there is no way to assess the credentials or experience of contributors to such public venues, a fact that participants must bear in mind. Nonetheless many practitioners have found these resources to be valuable.

Not surprisingly, manufacturers of products for the healthcare industry see in the Internet an opportunity to influence the delivery of medical care and promote the use of their products. Pharmaceutical and equipment companies have web sites for their products, sponsor "free" CME, and place advertisements on medically oriented web sites.

The availability of numerous Internet resources—of variable quality and bias—raises the question: How useful is all of this information to the average practicing physician? Most practitioners are extremely busy and have limited time for reading; viewed from their perspective, the Internet may represent a vast universe of information that they have no time to explore. Targeted e-mail discussion lists; efficient, physician-oriented search engines; and discriminating use of literature search engines will make the Internet an increasingly valuable medical knowledge resource in the future. Recently published guidelines that offer a "common sense" approach to evaluating the quality of medical information on the Internet[15] may enhance the future utility of the medium for physicians.

The Physician-Patient Relationship

Perhaps the area where the Internet has made the greatest impact on physicians in their daily practice relates to the unprecedented ease with which patients can obtain vast amounts of information on virtually any topic in medicine and healthcare. Patients are taking advantage of this convenient access to information to research their conditions, converse with others who have similar illnesses, and investigate providers and alternative therapies. Ever more frequently, patients arrive at their physician's office with reams of material downloaded from the web, demanding a new level of discussion based on these piles of unfiltered information.

This phenomenon symbolizes and contributes to a growing trend in healthcare today: the "consumerization" of medical care. Patients increasingly participate in and expect to share responsibility for all aspects of their care, including the medical decision-making process. The public is now more skeptical than previous generations and more likely to demand both qualitative and quantitative information—about their providers, procedures, medications, healthcare facilities, health plans, and outcomes. The Internet has accelerated this process.

The trend of the self-educated patient presents both opportunities and challenges for physicians. The traditionally minded physician may feel threatened by the patient who shows up carrying the latest asthma care guidelines from AHCPR. However, the physician who considers himself or herself a collaborator and partner with the patient in his or her care welcomes the motivated patient. Better-educated, more responsible patients are likely to assume an active role in their care management, and the physician can rely upon such a patient to monitor himself or herself diligently and follow up on identified needs in an appropriate fashion.[16] This is becoming increasingly important, given the shift from inpatient to ambulatory treatment of many conditions and the increasing emphasis upon cross-continuum care management. Improved communication between physicians and patients should lead to better outcomes.[17]

Another challenge presented by the Internet is that of information overload and the complete absence of quality control. One can post virtually anything on the Internet; it has become a sort of public press, devoid of editorial oversight. Numerous sources of information on medicine and health are available, from medical professional societies and government agencies to pharmaceutical companies and disease-specific patient support groups. The level at which the material is developed and researched varies accordingly, as do the completeness, bias, and timeliness of information.

Internet users have no way to ascertain the credentials or qualifications of contributors to most discussion groups. Some site sponsors voluntarily adhere to and publicize the Health on the Net Foundation Code of Conduct (www.hon.ch/HONcode/Conduct.html) for healthcare sources on the Internet.[18] In addition, the government is starting to review the online behavior of some web participants; for example, the FDA has investigated fraudulent drug-marketing claims on the Internet over the past two years and has issued consumer-oriented guidelines for understanding the information (vm.cfsan.fda.gov/~dms/fdonline.html).

How can physicians address these challenges? First, practitioners must develop a basic awareness of the kinds of resources available on the Internet, and the strengths and limitations of these sources. Physicians should help patients distinguish quality sources from others; this is particularly true in the specialties that deal with chronic illness, as providers in these areas will undoubtedly become familiar with some of the more frequently visited sites—if only by word of mouth from their patients. Physicians may wish to include references to some of the more reputable sites in their patient education literature.

Some physicians elect to create their own web sites, generally for marketing purposes, that can guide patients to recommended information sources using hypertext links. The value of such sites for marketing varies according to the physician's specialty; practitioners who advertise elective procedures are likely to derive more benefit from a web presence than the average primary care physician. Many reference sources exist for physicians who wish to establish their own web sites.[19]

Communications Between Doctor and Patient

The use of e-mail is growing rapidly; it has been estimated that between 15 and 20 percent of physicians were e-mail users as of 1997.[20] Although most use is directed toward administrative functions, an increasing number of providers find themselves corresponding with patients over the Internet. Anyone who has recently attempted to contact a physician by telephone will immediately grasp the value of e-mail for patient-physician communication.

The asynchronous nature of e-mail communication serves to lower the barrier to patient-provider contact; patients are likely to be less hesitant to ask follow-up questions of the physician following an office visit when they know they will not be interrupting their doctor. E-mail can also be used by providers to offer patient education materials and reference resources, such as recommended URLs (as discussed earlier).

From the physician's point of view, there are distinct advantages to the use of e-mail over the telephone, in addition to convenience. E-mail automatically documents the patient-provider interaction, eliminating the need for paper reminder messages and providing a record of the encounter for future reference.

There are two principal sources of concern regarding physician–patient e-mail correspondence: confidentiality and medicolegal issues. Securing patient information from unauthorized review cannot easily be guaranteed, given the diverse range of e-mail and network systems in use by different organizations, and patients may choose not to share particularly sensitive information via e-mail. The literature does, however, hold at least one example of psychiatrists using the Internet for patient consultations.[21] Confidentiality requires that providers have a means of limiting access to their e-mail accounts; this can be difficult when, for example, a family shares an account.

The medicolegal issues are similarly complex. Messages from patients should be routinely printed and inserted into their paper records or incorporated into their electronic paperless records. Providers must be careful not to include patient-identifiable information in unencrypted correspondence and must be cautious in their choice of wording with patients, avoiding judgmental or critical remarks. These and other considerations are outlined in the guidelines of the American Medical Informatics Association (AMIA) for the use of electronic mail with patients.[22] There is to date little other guidance or legal precedent in this area.

Although it is prudent to be aware of these considerations, there is little doubt that patient-provider e-mail will continue to increase in popular use. Given the appropriate safeguards and policy implementation, physicians can successfully deploy e-mail in their medical practice, just as many have done for routine business use. Use of e-mail is, of course, not appropriate for urgent needs, and auto-response features can remind patients of this, as well as confirm receipt of a message. Many physicians, group practices, and integrated delivery networks have established web sites that offer patients the opportunity to communicate directly with physicians regarding clinical questions (e.g., hsc.virginia.edu/cmc/e-mailsrv.html, www.medhelp.org/, www.mediconsult.com).

The geographic limits of medical and legal responsibility pose another difficulty. What is the professional liability of a physician in Massachusetts giving medical advice to a patient from Missouri? Is the care occurring in one state, both states, or in neither state? These questions must be addressed in a comprehensive manner as society embraces this new method of communication.

Conclusion

The Internet is affecting the practicing physician today, albeit often through his or her patients. In the near future, the day-to-day impact of this medium will grow as physicians look to the Internet for patient-specific information, organizational guidelines, and medical knowledge bases. Perhaps the most profound effects of the Internet will be seen in the area of communication between physicians and patients. Better communication should translate to better care, and better care to better outcomes. Although many obstacles must be overcome, the Internet will make a significant positive contribution to the physician-patient relationship in the future.

Notes

1. Willard, K. E., J. H. Hallgren, B. Sielaff, D. P. Connelly. 1995. "The Deployment of a World Wide Web (W3) Based Medical Information System." *Proceedings of the Annual Symposium on Computer Applications in Medical Care* 771–75.
2. Cimino, J. J., S. A. Socratous, and P. D. Clayton. 1995. "Internet as Clinical Information System: Application Development Using the World Wide Web." *Journal of the American Medical Informatics Association* 2 (5): 273–84.

3. Reddy, S., M. Niewiadomska-Bugaj, Y. V. Reddy, H. C. Galfalvy, V. Jagannathan, R. Raman, K. Srinivas, R. Shank, T. Davis, S. Friedman, B. Merkin, and M. Kilkenny. 1997. "Experiences with ARTEMIS: An Internet-Based Telemedicine System." *Proceedings of the AMIA Annual Fall Symposium* 759–63.

4. Halamka, J. D., and C. Safran. 1997. "Virtual Consolidation of Boston's Beth Israel and New England Deaconess Hospitals via the World Wide Web." *Proceedings of the AMIA Annual Fall Symposium* 349–53.

5. *Inside Healthcare Computing.* 1998. 8 (18): 1–3.

6. Kittredge, R., U. Rabbani, F. Melanson, and O. Barnett. 1997. "Experiences in Deployment of a Web-Based CIS for Referring Physicians." *Proceedings of the AMIA Annual Fall Symposium* 320–24.

7. Sylvestri, M. F. 1996. "Health Care Informatics: The Key to Successful Disease Management." *Medical Interface* 9 (5): 94–6, 98–9.

8. Goldstein, D. 1997. "Internet-Based Disease and Demand Management." *Managed Care Interface* 10 (10): 50–2.

9. Caramella, D. 1996. "Teleradiology: State of the Art in Clinical Environment." *European Journal of Radiology* 22 (3): 197–204.

10. Moncur, J. T., J. M. Rosen, S. Zhu, and F. M. Limonadi. 1997. "Medical Electronic Link MEL: Providing Telemedicine on the World Wide Web." *Stud Health Technol Inform* 39: 328–33.

11. Siwicki, B. 1996. "Intranets in Health Care." *Health Data Management* 36–47.

12. Fotsch, E. 1997. "Extending and Enhancing Existing Information Systems Using Internet-Based Technologies." *Healthcare Financial Management* 32–33.

13. Elliott, S. J., and R. G. Elliott. 1996. "Internet List Servers and Pediatrics: Newly Emerging Legal and Clinical Practice Issues." *Pediatrics* 97 (3): 399–400.

14. Oyston, J. P., and J. G. Ascah. 1997. "The Value of the Internet to Anaesthetists." *Canadian Journal of Anaesthesia* 44 (4): 439–44.

15. Silberg, W. M., G. D. Lundberg, and R. A. Musacchio. 1997. "Assessing, Controlling, and Assuring the Quality of Medical Information on the Internet: Caveant Lector et Viewor—Let the Reader and Viewer Beware." *Journal of the American Medical Association* 277 (15): 1244–45.

16. Mechanic, D. 1998. "Public Trust and Initiatives for New Health Care Partnerships." *Milbank Quarterly* 76 (2): 281–302.

17. Bader, S. A., and R. M. Braude. 1998. " 'Patient Informatics': Creating New Partnerships in Medical Decision Making." *Academic Medicine* 73 (4): 408–11.

18. Benjamin, I., and J. W. Goldwien. 1998. "Oncology and the Internet." *MD Computing* 15 (4): 242–45.

44   *The Internet and Healthcare*

19. Borzo, G. 1998. "Home on the Web." *American Medical News* 41 (29): 24; Smith, R. P., and M. J. A. Edwards. 1997. *The Internet for Physicians.* New York: Springer-Verlag; Lowes, R. L. 1998. "WWW: Can Three Little Letters Spell Prosperity for Your Practice?" *Medical Economics* (Pediatrics edition, April): 46–52.
20. Kane, B., and D. Z. Sands. 1998. "Guidelines for the Clinical Use of Electronic Mail with Patients: The AMIA Internet Working Group, Task Force on Guidelines for the Use of Clinic-Patient Electronic Mail." *Journal of the American Medical Informatics Association* 5 (1): 104.
21. Johnston, C. 1996. "Psychiatrist Says Counseling via E-Mail May Be Yet Another Medical Use for Internet." *CMAJ* 155 (11): 1606–7.
22. Kane, B., and D. Z. Sands. 1998. "Guidelines for the Clinical Use of Electronic Mail with Patients: The AMIA Internet Working Group, Task Force on Guidelines for the Use of Clinic-Patient Electronic Mail." *Journal of the American Medical Informatics Association* 5 (1): 104–11.

4

Call Centers and
the Internet

John Odden

During the past decade, businesses of every size and type have
explored the power of the Internet, intranets, and extranets. As
fear of computers has eroded, these ever-changing technologies
have been used to expand intellectual capital, advance the speed
and quality of communication, and facilitate greater connectivity
among all the stakeholders in organizations. Healthcare, in the
midst of drastic redesign, has been no exception. Its CEOs have
recognized the value and potential of Internet-related technology,
and they have poured significant time, energy, and capital into
leveraging it.

For health plans, the appeal of Internet/intranet/extranet
technology is especially broad. Payors can use it to slash the high
price of administration and simplify its processes. Providers can
use it to share information with each other, conduct quick and
inexpensive research, and improve the outcomes of clinical care.
Consumers, the group with which today's health plans are most
concerned, can use it to educate themselves about disease prevention, fitness, and treatment plans.

With these benefits now being realized in many organizations, healthcare is beginning to see the effect the Internet can have
within their respective organizations. Now we must take the next

step: exploring what it can do in tandem with other technologies. The call center, a vital part of today's customer-focused health-care environment, is a good launching pad for this next phase of progress. Both its benefits and its limitations make it an ideal partner for Internet technology.

Call Centers and the Internet: Justifying a Merger

At any given time, both call centers and the Internet (i.e., a web application or web server) are serving a mix of members, providers, and employers in a healthcare organization. The call center and the Internet service may share some content (e.g., procedures, guidelines, frequently asked questions [FAQs]), but these two entities must be interconnected to maximize efficiency and quality. Where healthcare transactions are concerned, one is often incomplete without the other.

Call centers, for example, aim to transform the way transactions are made. In healthcare, as in other industries, a full service call center that makes appropriate use of the latest technology is a bridge to customer satisfaction. However, without a supplementary technology, these centers will sometimes fall short of consumers' expectations. Because it is not economically practical to build a call center large enough to give each customer *immediate personalized* service at any time of the day, some callers will be unwilling to use the center in the future. Use of the Internet would help overcome this obstacle, delivering a rich multimedia experience and an affordable way to provide acceptable levels of service during peak periods.

Just as the Internet can help reduce a call center's frustration factor, call centers can help overcome some of the Internet's limitations. A provider looking for lab results or a member trying to understand the copay for a procedure by looking at a web application may or may not find the needed information quickly and successfully. If a call center is available and the agents are properly trained, users who have hit roadblocks can call for assistance, solving the problem quickly and minimizing customer frustration.

Business Applications and Benefits

The business applications of an Internet/call center merger are, of course, primarily customer service–oriented. When properly designed and implemented, they have the power to change the way many routine transactions are handled. Specific examples include:

- *ER triage and authorization.* Steers members to a contracted or in-network ER rather than an out-of-network ER; also allows members to receive immediate access and treatment in preapproved ER facilities. In addition, it can either advise a physician office visit or describe self-care and monitoring.
- *Appointment scheduling.* Enlists trained agents to ensure that members receive their preferred appointment times, locations, and providers.
- *Provider referral.* Gives patients fast access to any specialty provider they may need.
- *Advice lines.* Give members information and self-care advice, assisting them as much as possible, short of an in-person discussion.
- *Pre-admit capabilities.* Collect ID and payment arrangement so that hospital check-in is streamlined and minimized.

As this list indicates, an Internet customer service web application has the potential to integrate and/or redirect many routine transactions out of the call center. Agents would then have more time available to respond to customers whose questions and concerns require the intervention of these agents, who are typically highly trained clinical staff. Many employers are starting to request report cards on customer service levels. Here, Internet applications can demonstrate significant productivity increases for those customers who like to use the web.

A well-designed Internet customer service application can quickly differentiate between questions that can be handled electronically and those that require human intervention (i.e., a connection to the call center). Customers are likely to feel more empowered when they can get an answer to their question quickly on the Internet and even "bookmark" that information so that they can easily access it again in the future.

Newer technology solutions like computer telephony integration (CTI) can provide a "call me" button that can be put on a healthcare organization's web page. With proper planning and deployment, the "call me" button can reserve an appropriate call center agent. The agent can then originate a call from the call center to the customer, display specific customer information on the agent's workstation, and view the web page that the customer is already browsing. If users experience difficulty, they click on the "call me" button and their call is transferred to an appropriately skilled agent.

Conversely, if a customer is talking to a call center agent and the answer is a lengthy block of information available on the web, that customer might better appreciate the alternative of viewing the answer over the Internet. He or she could easily print the entire response or selected passages in hard copy form. Many times, the call center agent can point the customer to the right page on the web server, so no material will have to be faxed, printed, or mailed to the customer.

These types of opportunities to connect customer service tools are both real and achievable, but they require careful planning and implementation. As the Internet emerges as part of the strategy for customer service, the plans for Internet service and call centers need to be coordinated. For the growing number of customers who prefer to access information through the Internet, the integration of call centers and Internet technologies is essential.

Taking Action: Essential Tasks and Potential Pitfalls

Merging and integrating the Internet with call centers is a highly desirable way to maximize the benefits of both technologies. How, then, can healthcare organizations implement such a strategy? The following is a high-level planning approach to achieving this objective.

Lay the Groundwork

Before project design can start, the organization must answer several preliminary questions. Who should be part of the project team? When should vendors be involved? What sort of timeline should be established, and what kind of approach should be taken? Who will be the project's "sponsor" or "champion"?

Assembling a well-rounded design team is the first step. Resources with call center and Internet skills and experience will be essential. The team should consist of a project sponsor/facilitator, content authors, a digital artist, a web developer, and several call center developers and integrators. Each member will have a unique and vital function. Call center resources can address metrics and efficiency and define the ways that an agent intervention can best help a customer whose request arrives for service via the Internet. Internet developers and content authors can suggest which kinds of information and formats might be offered from the web domain to call center agents and callers. Digital artists can visualize and simplify content into an attractive and efficient presentation that will encourage users to return.

Once the team is assembled, members should agree on the approach they will take to making the project succeed. In general, a reengineering approach will need to be incorporated in projects as complex as these. This is especially true with these technologies, because the differences in performance objectives between call centers and the Internet necessitate different sets of business processes and models. The Internet domain, in which content and knowledge rule, emphasizes completeness, accuracy, and a self-paced investigation. The call center dynamics, however, concentrate on rapid evaluation of requests and ultra-efficient responses to queries. Integration of both models needs to be addressed from a reengineering perspective if the resulting capabilities are to serve their respective stakeholders.

During the early discussions about methodology, the team should decide whether they should test the project with a pilot before large-scale implementation begins. Healthcare organizations tend to embrace pilots, mostly because they provide for learning and allow a better opportunity to design an efficient roll-out. If, however, the organization has significant experience with projects of this scope and complexity, a pilot may not be necessary.

Throughout these early planning stages, it is important to remember that successful call centers often start small and build slowly. One example is Sisters of Charity HealthPrompt in Houston, a call center that handles provider referral and dispenses information through an advice nurse line. Though marketing was the major catalyst behind its launch five years ago, demand management has become the top priority as the center has expanded. Since 1993, it has grown from three to four professional full-time employees (FTEs) to 25 FTEs, including more than 15 RNs. Currently, it handles approximately 12,000 calls per month.

Consider RAD Methodology

We have analyzed a series of projects conducted with customer service agents working in healthcare call centers. These revealed that a modified rapid application development (RAD) methodology can be very successful in creating a superior Internet-based customer service application. If there is sufficient infrastructure in place (i.e., an intranet, Internet web sites, call centers, call center servers, and databases) to support such a high-performance methodology, organizations should take advantage of these circumstances.

In this approach, the most successful agents in a call center guide a RAD project team in creating web pages that speed and simplify the task of responding to customers. These agents will tell the development team how to partition and organize the reference material so that it responds to the most crucial customer requirements or concerns, and they will indicate the best ways to access the balance of the information. Using the RAD process, the task of the development team becomes understanding what customer services agents need and creating a series of templates that will allow them to quickly and efficiently capture that information.

Identify Content Requirements

As the Internet industry continues to charge ahead with innovations and improvements, the project team will find it especially difficult to develop solutions with a long shelf life. If a call center technology architecture locks in particular Internet products, formats, or vendors, it will probably be obsolete in just a few months. Therefore, the major challenge for project designers is to decouple that architecture from the specific applications and functions.

A crucial step toward this goal is building common information content (i.e., knowledge bases) for call centers and Internet customer service applications. The information requirements in the call center and the Internet customer service platform tend to be very comparable, and it may be possible to develop both at once. This strategy for sharing content and tools will enable rapid replacement of Internet software and content. Healthcare organizations that embrace this approach will also be able to harvest their investment in legacy systems and future systems for years to come.

Simplify Content Design

The layout of web sites is another major consideration. Web site information must be readable and easy to understand. Icons, color, and even animation can make the site more pleasurable to visit and navigate, and the team should experiment periodically with different design options until it finds the best approach.

Measure Success

After the project is implemented, it is important to document and record the number of customers using this new opportunity to obtain self-service. Tracking activity on the Internet customer service application will indicate the quantity and distribution of all calls or transactions by day of week, time of day, and transaction type. To provide a complete profile of this new form of largely automated self-service transaction, the organization should also document the use of the "call me" feature or provide agents with activity reports to track agent work in support of Internet-originating transactions.

Any organization that values customer service, quality, and satisfaction highly enough to integrate the call center with Internet service resources will want to take this final step of tracking and responding to the volume of Internet-based transactions. It is a way to measure the success of the project and decide whether improvements are needed.

Future Considerations

Though many organizations have only recently selected a call center product vendor, the knowledge intensity of healthcare customer service means it is already time to look ahead to the Internet tools and formats that will soon be popular. Call center vendors, for example, are offering the capability of placing "call me" or "request call back" buttons on public web pages. These features will clearly earn a place in healthcare applications, where the complexity or confidentiality of information often prevents it from being delivered over the public Internet. Similarly, the Internet products that support e-commerce will eventually qualify for selected applications in healthcare. Considering the cost savings that may be available in e-commerce, these products should be monitored for suitability in healthcare applications.

Clearly, the call center industry has seen the opportunity to integrate telephone-based customer service with the Internet as a new and powerful delivery channel. In fact, much of the call center/Internet integration capability is running ahead of most organizations' abilities to deploy it. CIOs will need to establish a vision and architecture that maximizes the benefits of these new opportunities to improve customer service.

5

The Evolving Internet
Steve Ditto

Many fortunes have been lost and entrepreneurial spirits crushed by the belief in the cruel adage that building a better mousetrap will attract droves of customers. From the time Alexander Graham Bell invented the telephone more than a century ago through the introduction of the television and personal computer, new communications technologies have required several critical success factors to evolve from early promise to widespread success. These include

- commercially viable programming;
- adequate distribution facilities;
- standardized and interoperable systems;
- attractive cost structures; and
- a critical mass of consumer acceptance.

Quite often, these success factors are dependent on one another, a situation that leads to a growth-hindering "chicken-or-the-egg" dilemma. However, when these success factors become available simultaneously, explosive growth and widespread acceptance are possible.

In the case of the Internet, four significant trends have converged and served as an explosive catalyst leading to rapid widespread acceptance:

1. the availability of Internet-based software (i.e., web browsers and HTML authoring tools) that makes it possible for almost anyone to publish, access, and share information in standard formats;
2. the widespread availability of Internet service providers enabling cost-effective access to the Internet from any home or business regardless of geographic location;
3. the development of Internet-based software standards that greatly simplify and standardize computer connectivity and interoperability; and
4. the proliferation of personal computers into businesses and homes, enabling access by millions of potential users.

The convergence of these trends, coupled with the availability of interesting and valuable web programming content, has been the primary driver behind the current phase of explosive Internet growth. Interest in the web and its ability to enable new business opportunities and enhance communications will continue to keep the Internet on a steady growth trajectory. However, the next phase of growth is likely to come from new market forces interested in having the Internet evolve from a byzantine web of interconnected computers to an information superhighway capable of supplanting other technologies and enabling innovative and profitable new applications.

The Allure of the Internet

All communications technologies have inherent technical limitations that may affect their ability to deliver business applications. For example, television can broadcast a high-quality video picture to large audiences, but it is severely limited in the number of channels that can be transmitted and by the geographic area that can receive the signal without significant interference. Consequently, television networks must focus on developing programming that has broad market appeal and that can attract mass advertisers who are able to afford the high cost of commercial time.

The advent of cable television significantly increased the number of available channels and gave rise to entirely new programming sources able to "narrowcast" to more focused audiences (e.g., MTV, ESPN, Home Shopping Network). Although the cable channels may have less appeal to some mass market advertisers, they are economically attractive to niche advertisers who can maximize the return on a relatively modest advertising investment. Ultimately, the business application of television technology is limited by the one-way, noninteractive nature of broadcasting, characteristics that make it unsuitable for delivering innovative applications like individually customized programming on demand or two-way interactive video. Equally important is the fact that the limited number of television channels limits the number of programming options, thereby creating significant competition for channel access, raising the cost of creating commercially viable programming, and erecting high barriers to entry into the programming industry.

In contrast to television, the Internet has traditionally been viewed as a two-way data communications technology that allows anyone to produce and self-publish programming content and allows anyone interested in such content to seek out and search for it. This ability to serve as a vast collection of electronic information is both the boon and the bane of the Internet. Many users of the Internet are drawn in by the opportunity to find interesting, valuable, or pertinent information, but some are discouraged by the time and effort required because of the inefficiencies of Internet search, index, and review.

The developers of Internet content, particularly those providing commercially oriented content directed at potential customers, have been equally frustrated by their inability to attract Internet users to their sites. "If you build it, they will come" has proven to be a fruitless marketing approach, and the likelihood of going undiscovered in the vast maze of online resources is high.

Even many sophisticated mass-market advertisers have found Internet marketing to be difficult thus far. Despite the now-ubiquitous presence of Internet addresses in most print and television advertising today, most Internet marketing efforts have yielded minimal results. However, as is often the case, frustration has become the inspiration for invention as "push" technology, a new and innovative approach to delivering Internet content, takes hold.

The push concept was pioneered by Pointcast, which developed a unique PC screensaver software program that periodically received information from Internet content providers and displayed it only when a user's PC was idle. A much more active and engaging form of push technology is now being incorporated by Microsoft and Netscape into their browser and server software. This will enable any Internet content provider to push information to a user's PC.

Using the unique push distribution capabilities of the Internet, content providers can develop push programs and entire push channels containing broadcast programming that has the mass appeal of television or radio, narrowcast programming to an unlimited number of niche audience subsegments traditionally served by magazines and newsletters (e.g., everything from astronomy to zoology), and microcast programming directed to specific populations (e.g., the physicians of XYZ Healthcare Corporation).

Although push technology has been hampered by current national bandwidth limitations, this unusual communications capability is still probably far from dead. The development of the necessary bandwidth for the Internet to act as a medium capable of broadcasting feature-rich programming channels (sometimes in competition with traditional media) has attracted the interest of some large and well-financed organizations, including

- traditional television and print media companies (e.g., NBC, CNN, ESPN, *Wall Street Journal*) that want to provide complementary services over the Internet; and
- new media companies (e.g., Microsoft, C Net) that want to provide access to new interactive programming content (e.g., multimedia encyclopedias, online multimedia magazines, interactive video games).

Searching the Information Superhighway

The Internet is a vast and rapidly growing repository of electronic information. However, current search and directory tools make finding information difficult and time-consuming. This problem will only get worse, as some predictions set the number of web pages in excess of one billion pages by 2000. In response, new applications commonly known as intelligent agents or personal assistants are being developed to continually search the Internet for information relevant to the user's profile.

Intelligent agents use a variety of techniques to "learn" what users consider relevant. The learning techniques range from simple approaches like interest filters, which use questionnaires about users' interests to refine the searches, to self-teaching artificial intelligence engines that monitor the information users read on the Internet to develop an interest profile. An interesting variation is the development of interest filters based on input from others having similar interests. In this variation, the intelligent agent asks the user to rate the quality and applicability of information and then compares those ratings to the ratings of others, whom the user may or may not know, to develop virtual special interest groups. When someone else within the user's virtual special interest group provides a high rating on new information, the intelligent agent will automatically monitor and retrieve the information for review.

The opportunity for using these tools to increase intellectual capital development in healthcare is immense. Intelligent agents used on corporate intranets can radically change the way and speed at which information is shared. As an example, in a newly integrated, growing, or distributed IDS, it is impossible to know who knows about, is interested in, or should be made aware of certain information. Using intelligent agents and group filtering, an update on trends in disease management might be distributed by means of a corporate intranet, both to the respective clinicians and to others who have shown recent interest. These might include the CEO who has been looking at emerging delivery practices, or the newly hired director of IT who developed an interest in disease management when working for a previous employer.

Search engine companies have developed a type of software, alternatively known as spiders or crawlers, that continually search the Internet for new information that can be categorized and indexed for searching and retrieval purposes. As legacy applications become more web-enabled, it will be possible for future spiders to search applications for a wide variety of information that has been "locked" away. For example, today it is very difficult to identify, capture, and integrate the information from the many different systems (e.g., ADT, lab, radiology, pharmacy) required to provide physicians with an integrated view of patient care across episodes and delivery sites. However, spider technology, coupled with suitable security mechanisms, could be used to seek out patient information, and web standards could be used to integrate and present information to a physician workstation. This approach could also aid in the development of important databases. The information from the search could be funneled into a master patient index (MPI), which would speed and enhance subsequent searches. The search information could also be abstracted to populate a longitudinal clinical data repository.

Opportunities on the Information Superhighway

Given both the low entry barrier to developing Internet content and the Internet's inherent multimedia capability to deliver text, audio, and video, Internet programming will become available in every format imaginable, from both traditional and new programming sources. Although the traditional communications media of radio, newspapers, magazines, and television will not be toppled overnight by these developments, no medium of information distribution will remain unaltered. Several changes are possible.

Radio

The effect of these developments on the radio industry will be broad and sweeping. Current radio stations (e.g., KRBE in Houston) are seeking to broaden their geographic coverage by means of the Internet; meanwhile, new Internet-only stations will be able to target specific niche audiences or provide a "digital jukebox" service of unlimited music selections on demand. Audio selections will be supplemented by print and video content and advertising. Record companies will be able to bypass the middlemen and distribute directly to the consumer. New music bands will have an affordable outlet for self-publishing their music, and new talk-radio opportunities will develop. The number of commercially viable traditional radio stations will dwindle, but the number of Internet stations will probably skyrocket because anyone will be able to become a broadcast mogul or disk jockey.

Within the healthcare industry, it will be possible for businesses to take advantage of these developments by producing and hosting healthcare talk shows and forums, providing patient education, delivering continuing medical education, developing dictation and transcription services, and holding interactive "wireside" chats between employees and management.

Newspapers

Some newspapers are seeking to broaden their geographic coverage with the Internet (e.g., *Wall Street Journal, San Jose Mercury News, Houston Chronicle*), and news service providers (e.g., Reuters, Dow Jones) are providing customized news selections on demand.

Newspapers will broaden their appeal by using the multimedia capability of the Internet to provide more detail to interested readers or complementary audio and video clips. This merging of different media types will compel newspapers into partnerships or mergers with other newsgathering organizations such as television stations. The current trend of newspaper consolidation will continue, although local and niche newspapers will be able to flourish given the low cost of Internet distribution.

Within the healthcare industry, it will be possible for businesses to take advantage of these developments by distributing customized healthcare industry news to employees, creating custom healthcare content for inclusion in electronic newspapers, and distributing healthcare newspapers and newsletters to consumers and patients. Leading organizations will use these mechanisms to capture and disseminate information from both internal and external sources. This will substantially increase the intellectual capital and productivity of their employees.

The current inability to easily download full-motion video images and display large screen sizes limits changes in this area. However, these limitations will be reduced in time through greater Internet transmission capacity, advances in video compression and processing, the availability of wide-screen television, and new efforts to integrate television and the Internet, such as WebTV.

Magazines

Many leading magazines have already adopted the Internet as a natural way of broadening their distribution network (e.g., *Business Week, Conde Nast Traveler, Forbes*). At the same time, new online magazines (e.g., *C Net, Wired*) are using the distribution capabilities of the Internet to enter the publishing market.

Like newspapers, magazines will broaden their appeal by using the multimedia capabilities of the Internet to provide additional detail, hot links to other relevant sites, and audio and video clips. Magazines will be forced to develop video production capabilities. In fact, significant synergy is already being achieved by companies like Discovery Communications, Inc., which successfully combines elements of magazines, television, and Internet programming with tie-ins to both traditional retail and electronic commerce.

Within the healthcare industry, businesses will be able to take advantage of these developments by creating and distributing customized healthcare magazines for employees. Significant opportunities exist to provide a wide range of consumer-oriented prevention, wellness, fitness, dietary, and self-care information directly to consumers. As with newspapers, current difficulties in downloading and displaying full-motion video images will be addressed by greater Internet transmission capacity and advances in video compression and processing.

Television

Perhaps Internet broadcasting holds more promise for the television media than for any other group. Despite current deficiencies in the ability of the Internet to provide broadcast-quality video, most of the major networks (e.g., NBC, CNN, ESPN) have begun positioning to provide Internet content. The Internet offers a means to remove the shackles of traditional television technology by providing a worldwide audience 24 hours a day.

Like newspapers and magazines, television can broaden its appeal using the multimedia capabilities of the Internet to provide even more detail to interested viewers and to perhaps shed its reliance on "sound bites." This merging of different media types will drive television networks into partnerships or mergers with other organizations, such as magazines and software companies. Microsoft and NBC are already testing this approach in their MSNBC venture, which successfully combines elements of television and Internet programming.

Additionally, the new delivery capabilities of the Internet hold much promise for advertisers, who will be able to offer customized advertising directed to specific niche audiences. Because it will be possible to know who is subscribing to a particular channel, Internet-based advertising can be customized to the potential buying habits of an individual viewer (e.g., offer a luxury vacation to the south of France for the CEO who purchases a case of Lafitte Rothschild while watching the Fine Wine Connoisseur channel).

Within the healthcare industry, businesses will take advantage of these developments by creating custom healthcare content for inclusion in television programs, developing healthcare television programs, and distributing customized healthcare television programs to employees and patients. Significant opportunities exist to provide a wide range of consumer-oriented programming, patient education, CME, and organizational training.

The current limitations in downloading and displaying video images clearly constrain the delivery of such service in this area. As an interim step, Intel has recently introduced new Intercast technology, which merges and synchronizes traditional television programming with Internet content using a television card in a PC coupled with an Internet connection. These limitations will be reduced in time through other advances, mentioned earlier.

Critical Success Factors

Several critical success factors will need to be in place before widespread acceptance of the Internet as a mass communications technology is possible. These factors include commercially viable programming, adequate distribution facilities, standardized and interoperable systems, attractive consumer cost, and critical mass of consumer acceptance.

Of these success factors, the largest impediment to the next phase of Internet growth is the lack of adequate distribution facilities, which limits the type of programming (i.e., graphic images and real-time, broadcast-quality video) that can be offered. It is important to note, however, that these are the structural limitations of an immature technology that is being rapidly upgraded as its commercial appeal is understood and heightened.

The problems with Internet distribution facilities fall into two areas: (1) the wide area network (WAN) crisscrossing the globe, and (2) the local distribution networks, known as the "last mile," linking homes and businesses to the global network. Of these two problem areas, the easier to solve are the global network problems. This area is increasingly becoming the domain of the large international telephone companies, because they have significant fiber-optic cable capacity in place and the financial wherewithal necessary to upgrade their transmission equipment to the required capacities. Additionally, new fiber-optic technologies, such as higher-speed lasers and wavelength division multiplexing, promise to provide bountiful capacity in the future.

The much more vexing problem is the last mile, where old copper cables predominate and choke the flow of information to a mere dribble. Here, too, there are a number of promising developments. For businesses, the news is relatively good. Most local telephone companies, and many of their local access competitors, are building fiber-optic distribution networks through most major business districts and corridors. These new networks promise high-speed connectivity that can deliver the next phase of Internet programming directly to business customers.

For businesses off the beaten path and for home-based users of the Internet, the news is mixed. Deploying new fiber-optic cable to these areas is often difficult and cost-prohibitive. New wireless technologies directed at business connectivity are becoming available based on recent FCC actions to reallocate radio spectrum to provide high-speed local access service. New technologies for increasing data transmission speeds over telephone cables, such as digital subscriber link (DSL) technology, show promise but offer only a fraction of the speed of fiber-optic cable. Other technologies, such as cable modems that are designed to use cable television facilities rather than telephone facilities, also show promise but are hampered by traditional cable television system designs, which did not anticipate two-way communications.

Solving these last-mile distribution facility problems will be the key to gaining audience critical mass, attracting advertising dollars that will lower the cost structure to consumers, unleashing new commercially viable programming, and providing an attractive return on investment to the companies investing in network expansion. The transformation of the Internet into a global information superhighway is just a short mile away.

6

Trends in Healthcare Information Technology

Dean Arnold

To lead a healthcare organization into the next century successfully, healthcare professionals will need to adopt new and innovative ways of thinking about and using information technologies. Several trends are making information systems (IS) and information technology (IT) a critical factor in the healthcare environment. Debates over cost, access, and delivery will continue to evolve, and as solutions are put in place, greater efforts to manage quality, affordability, and longitudinal care will present new challenges. There is no question that the Internet presents many technological solutions to an industry seeking broader access to manageable information.

As the healthcare industry struggles to confront the changing landscape, two particularly significant trends have emerged. First is the movement from inpatient-focused, acute-care settings to a broader, more integrated delivery mechanism, resulting in the formation of IDSs. Second is the aggressive application of information technologies to ever-changing business strategies and objectives. Figure 6.1 illustrates these trends.

The advent of managed care has engendered a new breed of healthcare players. Everyone's role has changed, especially the hospital's. There is an increasing demand for information to

Figure 6.1   Trends in the Evolution of IDSs

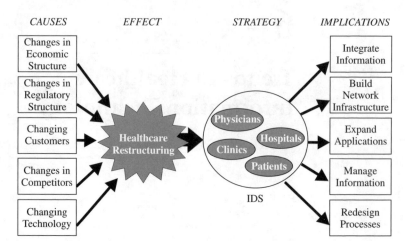

manage wellness, determine case-by-case costs, and allow providers to compete for the highest-quality treatment at the lowest
cost. Therefore, information systems must be used not only to
facilitate workload, but also to help compete in a new market that
is information-dependent.

The IDS

Currently, many independent care providers are organizing into
collections of delivery systems covering wide geographic areas
(Figure 6.2). It is predicted that the existing, highly fragmented
healthcare industry will consolidate into two or three IDSs per
market. As these new health systems emerge, the value of care
provided will increase through the development of integrated
processes and services—organizationally connecting networks of
physicians, multispecialist practices, clinics, hospitals, and other
care providers.

   One of the major tasks confronting an IDS is to coordinate
facilities, resources, operations, and information across both organizational and geographic boundaries. Furthermore, an IDS must
compete in the managed care arena by demonstrating the quality

Figure 6.2 Integration in Healthcare: Horizontal vs. Vertical

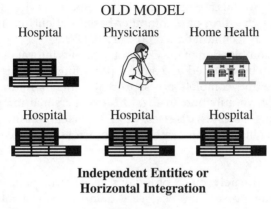

OLD MODEL

Hospital   Physicians   Home Health

Hospital   Hospital   Hospital

**Independent Entities or
Horizontal Integration**

NEW MODEL

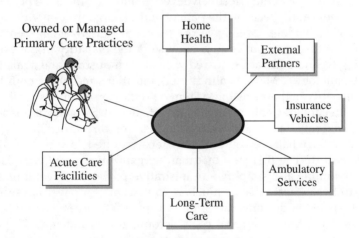

Owned or Managed
Primary Care Practices

Home
Health

External
Partners

Insurance
Vehicles

Acute Care
Facilities

Ambulatory
Services

Long-Term
Care

Vertically Integrated Delivery

of care it provides at competitive prices. The rapid development of IDSs has, therefore, created an enormous demand for a new generation of information systems.

The goal is to create an integrated system that enables seamless patient care. This means that from birth to death, the patient's information follows him or her throughout the system.

Furthermore, the patient is treated more effectively and more cost-effectively, because more and better information about that patient is available to the care provider at the point of service. This goal often takes the form of a computer-based patient record (CPR) supported by a clinical data repository (CDR).

The combination of the CPR/CDR allows information about a patient to be collected and stored, providing the clinician with immediate and complete access to that patient's information— for example, family and medical history, personal information, medications, illnesses, diseases, procedures, clinical images, and so on. This information can be viewed across multiple episodes of care, establishing a longitudinal view of the patient's clinical history.

Unfortunately, many of today's healthcare application systems do not possess the necessary data or level of integration required to support a "complete" CPR. Furthermore, data that do exist are not being effectively leveraged to maximize the possible benefits and effects on the patient and the organization. Information technology does have the potential to deliver big benefits to healthcare organizations because of the disparity in the existing technologies as compared with other industries and available technologies. Many healthcare organizations recognize both the disparity in their existing systems and the opportunities available for technology enhancements. In fact, most IDS organizations surveyed rank IT initiatives as one of their top three priorities.

So what are some of the steps required to move an IDS forward? The first step that many organizations are taking is to streamline and simplify administrative processes. Several recent studies indicate that as much as 38 percent of a physician's time is spent on administrative tasks (up to 50 percent for nurses), and that administrative costs account for as much as 25 percent of a typical physician's cost of service.[1] Information technology is often an effective weapon to neutralize these inefficiencies and reduce the administrative burden, lowering these costs. Opportunities for automating and restructuring administrative processes include online eligibility and benefit verification, automated payment processing, electronic claims submissions, centralized patient scheduling, attestation, and enrollment.

The second step—to many the most significant—is to enhance the clinical decision-making process. This is a fundamentally different approach than those undertaken to automate back-office operations, which typically focus on reducing expenses and handling increased capacity. Enhancing the clinical decision-making process through the integration of clinical information involves improving the quality of care by revising the traditional model of medical decision making: that is, adding information-handling capabilities to the hands-on clinical caregiver. Underlying benefits of this approach include reductions of lab requests and retestings, misdiagnoses, medical complications (e.g., drug interactions), and lengths of hospital stay, as well as increases in the delivery of preventive medicine, early interventions, and effective treatment plans.

For example, two studies in the *Journal of the American Medical Association* have shown that doctors using a highly integrated information system were able to find information about drugs, their side effects and potential interactions, as well as patient allergies and medical records—information that helped shape immediate treatment decisions.[2] A third study showed access to timely patient history information resulted in a significant reduction in medication errors.[3]

As these studies demonstrate, the use of highly integrated information infrastructures to support the IDS business model can provide caregivers with the necessary tools to improve decisions concerning diagnoses, treatments, and costs.

Integrating Information

Collecting, enhancing, delivering, and tracking data throughout the system are all vital information integration functions required to transform systemwide data into meaningful and useful information. Figure 6.3 depicts an information integration model.

The objective of information integration is to provide simple, flexible access to enterprise information. The strategies that support this objective include delivery of common user views, leverage of a network infrastructure to link users with required data, use of integration technologies to simplify system interfaces, and identification of standard integration toolkits. Certain technologies also promote access to enterprise information. They include a universal patient identifier (UPI), a CDR, and data warehouses. These initiatives play pivotal roles in integrating patient-related

Figure 6.3   Information Integration Model

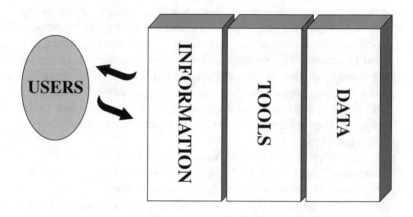

data, just as common user views of information provide simple access to enterprisewide information.

Tools and technologies are rapidly emerging to aggregate and store data that can later be accessed. Users can retrieve the data either prospectively, as in the case of the clinical data repository in which the care provider's slice of information is across a single patient, or retrospectively, in which case information is viewed across categories of data (e.g., multiple patients, physicians, contracts).

The data being integrated are also changing. Sources and types of data are taking on new forms, including speech recognition, handwriting entry, video, and imaging. A complete CPR will be a composite of data sources compiled from many points across the continuum of care.

With the use of these new sources and types of data, some technical and technology issues also emerge. Efforts to link to legacy application systems give rise to new requirements for access to information. Current and future applications and their associated data do not conform to the same set of standards. Thus, interfacing existing systems with new systems and enhancing the data extracted can present a very perplexing problem.

One of the more significant integration trends that have emerged in the past several years is that of connecting independently developed applications and systems through the use of "middleware" integration tools and technologies. One such middleware technology is message brokering. Often implemented through an application integration engine or gateway (AIE/G), message brokering acts as a logical hub that copies and resends messages to one or more destinations throughout a system. It is an intelligent transfer agent—a broker—between data sources and information destinations so that information flows are more easily accessed. AIE/Gs have been used quite successfully over the past several years as a means to interface ancillary applications such as laboratory and radiology information systems with the core patient accounting systems within a hospital or health system. Taking this technology a step further, many health systems are using message-brokering technology to implement key strategic functions such as the UPI and as a means to populate the clinical data repository and data warehouses.

An even more recent trend is to combine message brokering with Internet/intranet tools and technologies. This approach offers a fresh and aggressive method for collecting and presenting independent sources of data. Using a web browser can capture front-end sources of data (typically collected by means of an AIE/G) and provide a level of access ubiquity previously not allowable. The end user needs only to access a web browser to retrieve this information, which normally would have required a custom-developed application or changes to the existing application. Therefore, information can be combined and presented in new and innovative ways. For example, a large academic medical center in the Southeast has recently made nearly all its clinical documentation available online in the form of web pages. This conversion of information required many back-end systems to be interfaced (e.g., transcription systems, online documentation, patient accounting, and clinical systems), so that the information could be extracted and entered into a web server where the information could then be made readily available to a wide population throughout the medical center enterprise.

Likewise, information can also be collected by means of an interactive web page that can then be integrated into a data store such as the CDR or a data warehouse. A powerful capability of Internet-based integration solutions is the ability to provide *virtual* integration in the eyes of end users, where the data appear to be integrated, but in fact are not.

Tracking Systemwide Information

Patients, and the information associated with them, must be accurately and uniquely identified within the health system. This fact has given rise to the development of the UPI. The UPI not only uniquely identifies the patient but also provides integrated patient identification within healthcare application systems, thus establishing an index across heterogeneous application systems. This index acts as a thread running through the IDS's information infrastructure. Access to the patient's "thread" (i.e., UPI) and all the relevant and associated data should be included in it. Obviously, this technology is vital to the development of the clinical data repository and the CPR. For this reason, it is being aggressively pursued by many emerging health delivery systems and healthcare technology organizations. It is important to note that many of these data and technology standards, such as UPI, are still evolving. While accommodating this type of data is critical, the need for flexibility in their design cannot be overemphasized.

The mass of information flowing through a delivery network must also be managed and maintained. It is the role of information management to monitor and track the sources and destinations of data. Access control and information security are paramount concerns to ensure proper protection of data flowing through the system.

Transporting Information

As demands for healthcare information broaden and shift from hospitals to clinics to the home and back, data will be required to be transported outside of the hospital to various care settings. Network infrastructures are the primary tool for collecting, transporting, and delivering information through the system.

At the network infrastructure level, technologies are focused on ensuring that users can access information from anywhere at any time (i.e., network communications) and on promoting flexible computing platforms that leverage technology investments. Specific strategies focus on establishing computing standards, developing a suite of services for workstation utilization based on user profiles, enhanced network administration and management, and cooperative networking efforts across the system of care. The platforms on which information is collected or delivered are also changing. The mainframe-attached terminal is being replaced by high-end "intelligent" workstations that support a graphical user interface to applications and systems. However, a new technology entrant, the network interface device (NID) has recently emerged. Also referred to as the "thin client," network computer TR, or NetPC, this technology promises to strike a balance between the "dumb" terminals of the past and the current trend toward "intelligent" workstations. The former remains relatively inexpensive to purchase and maintain but has very limited capabilities, while the latter offers extensive and highly flexible capabilities but is expensive to purchase and maintain. By contrast, the NID, as currently conceived, has been designed around the Internet and takes advantage of the simplicity of a web browser. The result is an end-user device that offers advanced capabilities with a relatively low cost of ownership. Trade-offs, however, occur at the transport level because of the different infrastructure required. Specific implications include response time, fault tolerance, network support staff, and network hardware and software upgrades, particularly in respect to client/server as opposed to network PC approaches.

Additionally, the need for mobility has spurred the development of mobile computing devices such as laptop computers, hand-held clinical devices, personal digital assistants, electronic tablets, and similar gadgetry. Mobility, in turn, has generated a demand for wireless technologies. Because of the breadth and depth of the demands put on healthcare information systems, a combination of technologies is required to establish an enterprisewide computing model. The new model is based on a broadened vision of the traditional need for network-based computing. (See Figure 6.4.)

Specific network-based healthcare technologies are being used to extend information across the continuum of care. For example, telemedicine and its related derivatives, teleradiology, telepathology, telemonitoring, and tele–home care are extending the reach of healthcare practitioners. Information networks will never replace the practitioner or the relationship between patient and doctor. Instead, network technology will enhance the

Figure 6.4   An Enterprisewide Computing Model

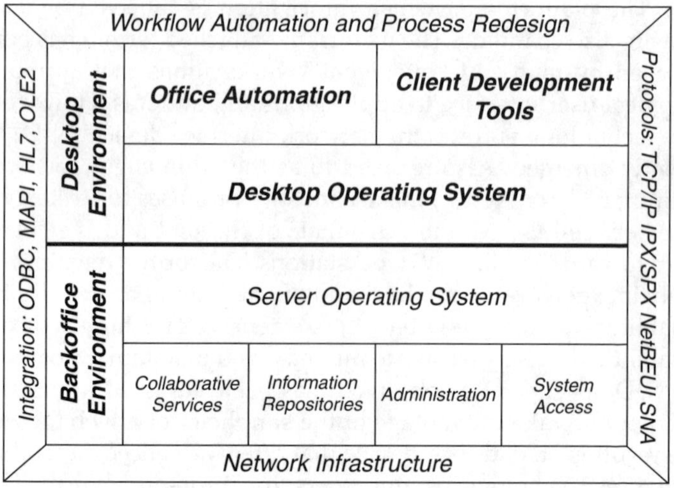

integration of healthcare services across the continuum of care and supply more meaningful information and decision support tools at the point of need. As integrated systems continue to extend their reach not only across the acute care setting but into primary, secondary, extended, and long-term care settings, networking is the vital link between end users and information.

Emerging Applications

Emerging application strategies are aimed at deploying systems that ensure sound clinical and business management. Where possible, systems are being employed to promote economies of scale, maximize software investments, and provide common data access and collection. Customization of products is typically being minimized to streamline systemwide implementation, administration, and support. Additionally, stable, proven vendor products are being deployed for core, or legacy, system functions (e.g., patient accounting, order communications). Additional strategies in this area include clinical system linkages to the CPR and system selection approaches ensuring informed decisions that support business and operational information gaps.

New applications that support new business strategies include the client/server computing model. These types of computer platforms have come to the forefront of emerging healthcare application development strategies. The inherent power and flexibility of client/server computing provide an effective computing and development environment by capitalizing on the underlying network infrastructure. Client/sever computing has spawned an array of object-oriented technologies that include object-oriented programming languages, object databases, object brokering, and object-oriented operating systems.

Although more traditional object-oriented technologies have been geared toward applications design and development that benefit programmers, new object-oriented technologies are quickly emerging that allow customer nonprogrammers to use prefabricated software components to develop complete customized solutions. Plugging components together empowers both IS professionals and users to deliver more focused, highly useful systems at reduced costs and time. Java and its cousin ActiveX are both web-based technologies that provide a framework for using these components over the Internet.

Although some experts predict the reduction, if not the demise, of client/server platforms as a result of the advent of web-based tools, many more believe these technologies present a new (and possibly better) paradigm for further client/server development and computing.

Conclusion

Over the past few years, the Internet has irreversibly changed the face of computing. As the demand for information increases, the Internet will continue to be leveraged and extended to deliver better and more meaningful information to an ever-expanding population of health information consumers.

The changing healthcare environment is rapidly shaping the information technology trends within our industry. IT strategies dependent on seamless integration of heterogeneous applications can be high-risk approaches and thus require expert management. Information integration, on the other hand, is based on the premise that heterogeneity and change are inherent in the current healthcare environment and therefore inescapable. IDSs, in particular, require tremendous amounts of data to be integrated from a wide variety of sources across organizational as well as geographic boundaries. As a result, incorporating information technology into business processes and business strategies is one of the top three priorities for healthcare organizations today.

A properly integrated information infrastructure will provide users throughout an IDS (i.e., patients, physicians, caregivers, employers, and payors) access to meaningful clinical information through the CPR and the CDR. It will also provide accurate and reliable clinical information management. (See Figure 6.5.)

Although the task of integrating the very large and complex amounts of information contained within an IDS may seem overwhelming, new tools and technologies have emerged to meet this demand. Web-based tools and technologies are providing complementary healthcare IT functions that provide increasing

Figure 6.5   An Integrated Information Infrastructure

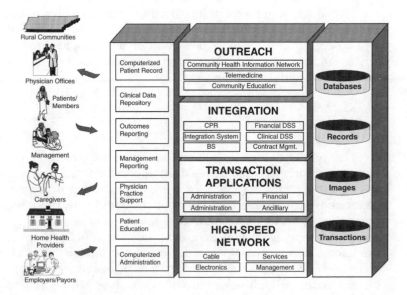

opportunities for the delivery of strategic applications such as the CPR and others. At the WAN level, public and private backbones will be scaled to meet the demands of IDS technologies through the deployment of such technologies as asynchronous transfer mode (ATM), synchronous optical transfer model (SONET), and synchronous digital hierarchy (SDH). In the coming years, the use of Internet and intranet technologies will prove a dynamic and flexible way to deliver healthcare information to end users.

Notes

1. LaRocco, L. 1994. "A Public Policy Framework for Our Nation's Health Information Infrastructure." *MD Computing* 11: 143–45.
2. Classen, D. C. 1997. "Adverse Drug Effects in Hospitalized Patients: Excess Length of Stay, Extra Costs, and Attributable Mortality." *Journal of the American Medical Association* 277 (4): 301–6; Bates, D. W., N. Spell, D. J. Cullen, E. Burdick, N. Laird, L. A. Petersen, S. D. Small, B. J. Sweitzer, and L. L. Leape. 1997. "The Costs of Adverse Drug Events in Hospitalized Patients." *Journal of the American Medical Association* 277 (4): 307–11.
3. Lesar, T. S., L. Briceland, and D. F. Stein. 1997. "Factors Related to Errors in Medication Prescribing." *Journal of the American Medical Association* 277 (4): 312–17.

7

Healthcare–Internet Technology Linkage
Paul Steinichen

Internet and web technologies are becoming the dominant standard for communicating information between different types of computing and networking systems. This networking platform can provide very valuable information resources to its users.

Generally, these information resources can be accessed at any healthcare institution by means of the Internet using various models. The simplest model requires no more than a PC with inexpensive software, a way of communicating outside of the institution, and a relationship with an ISP.

For example, a PC with Windows 98 and a web browser like Netscape Communicator can use a dial-out modem to communicate with an ISP like AT&T WorldNet. If the PC were connected to a local area network (LAN), then provisions could be made to allow the PC to communicate through the LAN to the ISP. This setup is relatively inexpensive and provides members of the organization with basic Internet/web access.

Many organizations now have intranet web sites for internal business and Internet web sites to share information with business partners and consumers. Web sites consist of at least one web server that provides content in a graphic manner. The web server may or may not physically contain all the data presented; advanced web sites typically collect dynamic data from other sources, such as intermediate data repositories, application interface engines, or original systems. Except for infrequently used web sites, most require day-to-day management with dedicated staff. Various support options are available to provide day-to-day support of web sites.

Intranets provide an information infrastructure link for organizing and presenting private and public information using the standard technologies developed on the Internet. An intranet model usually requires the institution to install a local intranet server. This server is functionally identical to an Internet server, except it services private information. Intranets are used to provide members of an organization with access to internal information by means of web technologies. For example, an intranet can be used to provide employees with on-demand access to their human resources files and information.

Intranet services are currently generating the most interest. This chapter aims to define the intranet model and the critical applications that the Internet/intranet model can address. Also included is a discussion on implementation of emerging Internet technologies, with particular attention to the following Internet/intranet issues:

The Internet/intranet as an information communications tool. An organization's intranet may become the information infrastructure that provides a standard for communicating information between dissimilar platforms within an organization.

Internet/intranet emerging technologies. The intranet infrastructure should allow an organization to leverage many of the emerging Internet technologies. These technologies range from the installation of super-servers and hybrid desktop devices, like thin clients, to the implementation of component-based systems.

Organizational and technical implementation issues. Implementing an intranet creates specific organizational and technical challenges, including issues like governance, network impact, and staffing.

Internet/Intranet as an Information Communications Tool

One of the biggest challenges facing healthcare IS departments is finding an efficient way to provide access to information. Typically, organizational data are located in various informational islands. For example, although much of the patient clinical data may be available through legacy systems, access to independent databases (i.e., decision support data, utilization review and quality assurance [UR/QA] statistics) and shared documents (e.g., policy and procedure manuals) is limited to individual desktop or network applications. Users must go through the cumbersome—and for the most part manual—process of moving between legacy software and network applications to gain access to the information from desktop computers. The Internet can provide the information infrastructure and tools necessary to give users a common desktop appearance for accessing all of the organization's data. Access to legacy systems or network databases can become transparent to the user through the use of buttons and search engines, which can swiftly take the user to the needed information with the help of standardized Internet tools. (See Figure 7.1.)

Figure 7.1   Internet/Intranet: An Information Communications Tool

External Communications	Internal Communications
• Home health agencies	• Pre-registration
• University medical centers	• Transportation requests
• Nursing homes	• Decision support data
• Patients' families	• Clinical notes
• Physician offices	• E-mail
• External vendors	• Internal inventory requests
• Rural health centers	• Policy and procedure manuals
	• OR scheduling
	• Lab results
	• Radiology results

Although no one organization has fully integrated all of its databases using Internet tools, national healthcare organizations have made substantial investments in this technology. For example, Columbia/HCA kicked off their intranet, referred to as "Koala," by creating online access to more than 150 training manuals, posting resumes and job opportunities, and creating an internal market for surplus equipment sales.[1] Kaiser-Permanente is also investing heavily in intranet technology; their IT spending was expected to increase by 12 percent in 1998, much of it devoted to Internet and intranet projects. Kaiser-Permanente Northwest is using an Internet browser to allow physicians access to medical records. In addition, human resources manuals, phone directories, and clinical practice guidelines are all available online. Upcoming enhancements include scheduling tools and hazardous chemical information.[2]

Creating online access to e-mail, policy and procedure manuals, employee newsletters, job postings, on-call schedules, and other static information is a great starting point for an intranet initiative. However, the real power of Internet technology lies in providing the infrastructure for integrating islands of information into collective sources of organizational knowledge.

Internet/Intranet Emerging Technologies

In many ways, the Internet is proving to be a great enabler of information networking. Thousands of product designers and users are continually suggesting, defining, and testing different ways to solve information-networking problems. Many of these problems are relevant to healthcare, and most of the solutions use standard, client/server, and object-based technologies.

The Internet can provide the means for moving information among networks, hardware platforms, and operating systems. Healthcare organizations that have expertise in the application of Internet technologies should be able to leverage such an Internet implementation. Thus, organizations with an Internet infrastructure will be able to react more quickly to information-networking innovations. This, in turn, should provide them a measurable competitive advantage.

Internet/Intranet Emerging Database Access Technologies

To provide the infrastructure and tools for accessing information, an organization must first provide the means to move information throughout the enterprise. Typically, initial infrastructure investments have been directed at the data network. However, once the data network has been stabilized, attention should be paid to the information network. An information network allows organizational data to flow where needed, regardless of the platform. When an intranet server with application programming interfaces (APIs) for database access is combined with a client browser, a significant portion of the infrastructure for information networking is in place.

Some of the major database interface standards currently in use are

- Netscape Server Application Program Interface (NSAPI);
- Microsoft's Internet Server Application Program Interface (ISAPI); and
- Oracle's Web Request Broker (WRB).

Enterprise Network Issues

Internet/intranet traffic can significantly affect enterprise network performance. However, most networking effects can be minimized through the implementation of logical and virtual LANs that are well designed and well managed. The placement of the servers within the networking hierarchy is critical. Typically, servers with high utilization should be placed higher on the network topology. Old rules of thumb for designing switching and virtual networks must be revised to take into account the tremendous amount of traffic moving through the enterprise.

The internal and external data security of any organization must also be considered and addressed. In general, security systems and devices should be installed to minimize potential security breaches. In particular, firewalls that provide application-layer security should be installed wherever there is an external connection to the public Internet. Typically, this firewall involves two pieces of hardware separated by a neutral zone.

Access to the intranet portions of organizational data from the Internet should also be protected by passwords. Data encryption should be used for the transmission of any information beyond an organization's direct control. Many of today's organizations are beginning to encrypt all information that is transmitted over all of these networks.[3]

Organizational and Technical Implementation Issues

An enterprisewide intranet with Internet access must meet the needs of three separate groups:

1. *End users.* The physicians, clinical and administrative staff, and executives who will ultimately use the intranet to obtain information

2. *Information sources.* The departments and information sources that provide data to other users

3. *IS support staff.* The intranet developers who create the applications that provide access between the information sources and the end users.[4]

A successful implementation strategy will meet the unique needs and expectations of each group. In addition, the implementation strategy should take into account four primary objectives:

1. *Individual and group access to data.* Ensuring that authorized access to vital clinical and operational data is available to users on demand

2. *Document management.* Providing shared and authorized access to internal documentation

3. *Desktop tools.* Providing access to tools such as word processing, spreadsheet applications, web browsers, and search engines

4. *Administrative control.* Ensuring that the Internet/intranet can be installed, configured, supported, and maintained from a central point.[5]

Three primary steps define the areas that should be considered prior to embarking on an Internet/intranet implementation.

Determine the organization's implementation readiness. A successful Internet/intranet implementation can fail before it even begins if the healthcare organization has operational impediments. For many healthcare organizations, preparing to implement Internet technology can require considerable reengineering to existing network systems. Any internal redesign efforts should be completed before tackling an Internet/intranet implementation.

Create an implementation oversight committee. A successful Internet/intranet implementation requires collaboration and support throughout the organization. End users should be encouraged not to see the project as "just one more IS project." The oversight committee should include representation from the three user groups previously identified. The primary objectives of the oversight committee should include

- establishing initial implementation goals and objectives;
- preparing the budget and the implementation timeline; and
- developing administrative controls and guidelines.

Define staffing requirements. Healthcare organizations must be careful not to overextend existing IS resources when implementing an Internet/intranet. Typically, existing staff are trained to support and maintain legacy software systems or LANs. As a result, this staff may not have the expertise or time necessary to design and support an Internet development effort. One alternative may be to outsource the entire operation.

Regardless of how an organization chooses to staff its Internet project, successful Internet deployment should include expertise in

- network communication and server management;
- performance and change management;
- web site design and publishing;
- strategic planning and monitoring;
- user training;
- documentation;
- help desk/user support;
- consulting (with departments to assist in designing the Internet to meet their needs, reengineering current information flows, etc.); and

- information engineering (i.e., personnel to maintain data dictionaries and act as advocates for the integration of information).[6]

Depending on which department is responsible for overall web site content, additional staff with specific expertise may be needed.[7]

Conclusion

Internet technology is opening doors for healthcare information management by means of the use of intranets. Common Internet tools like web browsers and search engines eventually may help resolve or minimize the problem of disparate databases. Instead of dealing with islands of information, healthcare professionals will be able to quickly access information from a common desktop platform.

The industry has yet to settle on all the standards for Internet tools, but progressive healthcare systems have already begun the implementation of this very robust technology. Investments in Internet/intranet technologies are expected to increase as more organizations enhance existing client/server networks with intranet capabilities.

Notes

1. Merrill, P. 1996. "BOTI Awards: Columbia Healthcare, Best Informational Intranet." *TechWeb* 1. techweb.cmp.com/cw/boti/col.html.
2. Mullich, J. 1996. "An Obvious Prescription." *PCWeek Online* 1–5, July 1. www.pcweek.com/builder/0701/01kais.html.
3. For additional information on security and firewalls, please refer to Chapter 9, "Issues and Concerns."
4. Horgan, T. 1996. "The Design and Implementation of a Corporate Web." From an online seminar series in *WebMaster Magazine*, Slide 12, 1996. www.cio.com/WebMaster/sem1tools.html.
5. Trowbridge, D. 1996. "Developing Intranets: Practical Issues for Implementation and Design." *Telecommunications Online* 3.
6. Horgan. (Undated). "The Design and Implementation of a Corporate Web."
7. Dreyer, S. M., and I. Fymat. 1996. "He Who Staffs Last." *WebMaster Magazine* 1, May. www.cio.com/WebMaster/wmarchive all. html.

8

Internet Frameworks
Kent Gray

From small family-owned businesses to multi-national conglomerates, organizations all over the globe are exploring ways to leverage Internet technology. Unfortunately, many have not accurately studied the ways that Internet technology (or any network technology, for that matter) can be used to effectively meet business goals and objectives. A framework is needed to

- determine how Internet/intranet solutions fit within the organization's business and technology strategies;
- identify potential opportunities for Internet-related solutions; and
- effectively apply Internet-related technologies within a healthcare setting.

Two frameworks are discussed below: a technology framework for aligning Internet-related products and services, and a life cycle methodology framework for implementing Internet technologies.

Technology Framework

The term "Internet technology" is becoming increasingly blurred. Virtually every computer vendor has come to incorporate Internet capabilities into its products and services; likewise, virtually every vendor promises some type of all-encompassing Internet solution that will require the replacement of existing systems. The question that must be asked, however, is exactly how any solution will fit within the organization's existing network infrastructure. It is important to have a model for categorizing Internet technology to illustrate the ways that the technology systems work together.

To better define the interrelationship of various technologies, First Consulting Group has developed a technology framework, pictured in Figure 8.1. Based loosely upon the OSI model, the model consists of nine major components:

1. *Physical infrastructure,* such as cabling and third-party access providers;
2. *Local area technologies,* including routers and switches;
3. *Wide area technologies,* which include remote routers and frame relay services;
4. *Remote access technologies,* including modems;
5. *Network services,* which represent messaging, file sharing, web services, and directory services;
6. *Network applications,* such as office automation and web browsers;
7. *End-user devices,* including workstations and peripherals;
8. *Shared resources,* such as servers and host systems; and

Figure 8.1   FCG Technology Framework Model

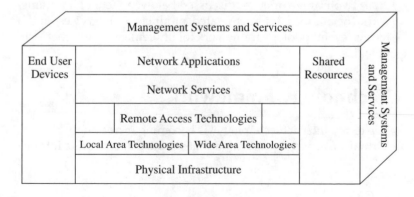

9. *Management systems and sources*, which include management and security tools for each of the previous components.

Using this simple model, where exactly do these Internet technologies fit in? Figure 8.2 illustrates some of the most prominent Internet technologies mapped to the model. Today, most Internet-enabling technologies have been concentrated in network services, network applications, and management systems and services. Examples of some of the technology categories follow.

End-User Devices

This category includes such items as traditional computers, network computers, and personal digital assistants (PDAs). The primary access method to the Internet remains the traditional PC; this

Figure 8.2   Technology Framework Model—Internet Technology Mapping

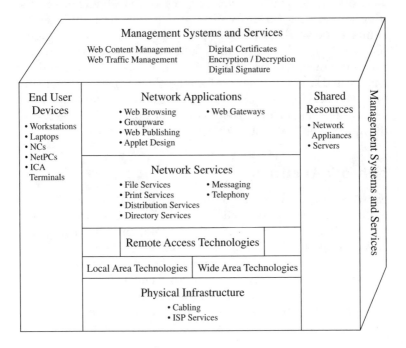

will continue for at least the next several years, especially for home users. Simple web terminals like WebTV will continue to increase their market share, but their limited functionality will keep total penetration low.

Shared Devices

Internet/intranet services can be provided on everything from desktop peripheral devices to large-scale mainframes. Some of the most progressive work is being done in the area of "network appliances," devices that perform a simple task with little start-up or maintenance cost. These devices may address the need for basic Internet services at remote healthcare facilities (e.g., clinics, private practices) without the cost of traditional NT/Novell/UNIX back-office IT solutions.

Network Services

Network services include web services, push technologies or distribution services, directory services (equating user and resource names to network addresses on a global basis), and messaging services. Network services are the key to providing web content across intranets and the Internet. Secure Internet-based commerce has created a new category of applications called commerce or merchant services, which allow organizations to sell goods and services to consumers as well as other businesses. This section of the model would also address EDI.

Network Applications

Network applications refer to those functions that typically span multiple business units, such as e-mail clients, web browsers, and office automation tools. Increasingly, companies are using web browsers and Java-based applications to access legacy system information. Depending on the scale of the project, these solutions can provide short-term and long-term benefit. For example, using web browsers can ensure immediate benefits, because they provide simple and relatively inexpensive interfaces to Internet resources. That same web browser, used in conjunction with a transcription project, could enable a physician to review and edit notes on multiple legacy transcription systems.

Management Systems and Services

These services include components like firewalls, web server monitoring, and network management and security tools. They will enable organizations to optimize value, reliability, and performance from the underlying network infrastructure by providing support staff with quantifiable performance metrics. Although these applications are generally perceived by the user community to be of low value, management and security solutions can be some of the easiest network service costs to justify. For example, service metering capabilities may be required for charge-back, which is particularly important because Internet communication will most likely involve partnering with customers, vendors, and Internet carriers.

Life Cycle Methodology Framework

Now that a technology framework has been defined, how are these technologies applied? The life cycle methodology developed by First Consulting Group (Figure 8.3) is an example of mapping products and services to business processes. The model divides business process into eight major "phases." Activities typical of all Internet-related projects are listed, along with common products, or "deliverables," of each phase.

Most healthcare organizations have developed an information systems strategic plan. A primary objective of such a plan should be identifying the way that information technology will be leveraged to meet current and future business objectives. Although there are a number of technical and operational issues related to achieving this objective, three key components are directly related to Internet/intranet solutions: an enterprise information architecture, an enterprise network architecture, and a security plan. Collectively, these documents should provide much of the governance for an Internet project design.

Figure 8.3   Internet Life Cycle Methodology

Phase	Assess	Strategize	Architect	Design	Select	Pilot	Implement	Operate
Activities	• ISP review • Content management review • Technology infrastructure review • Web traffic study	• Confirm business drivers • Establish IT direction • Identify/prioritize tactical projects • Establish timelines and interdependencies • Determine resource requirements	• Outline IT requirements • Develop framework • Define standards and guidelines • Develop technology roadmap	• Develop detailed functional and technical requirments • Distribute RFI (if required) • Develop design specifications • Outline implementation plan	• Develop RFQ/RFP • Evaluate responses • Negotiate contracts	• Confirm requirements • Establish success criteria • Build and test prototype/processes • Conduct pilot • Measure results/outcomes • Refine design (if required) • Finalize design and implementation plan	• Finalize implementation process • Procure products and services • Educate and train support staff and users • Configure and unit test • Install and system test • Finalize documentation	• Transition to ongoing support • Manage and administer production environment
Deliverables	• Intranet diagnostic review	• IT vision • Intranet/Internet strategy • Timeline • Resource estimates	• Intranet architecture	• Intranet content governance • Web site design • Implementation plan outline	• RFQ/RFP • Vendor recommendation • Signed contract/vendor agreement	• Pilot results • Final design documentation and implementation plan	• Documented production environment	• Support policies and procedures

Ongoing Project Management

• Status reports
• Project package
  • workplan
  • timeline
  • budget
• Team coordination
• Client communications
• Ensure quality and value

An information architecture defines relationships between the major data repositories of an organization. Healthcare advances in master member indexes and clinical repositories make an "information map" critical for extending information access to business partners. A comprehensive information architecture would define all the components (i.e., data, application, and network) necessary for electronic commerce, internal/external web sites, and remote access solutions. Internet/intranet demand is currently driving the information industry toward information architectures more reminiscent of a centralized host/terminal processing model than the client/server model made popular over the past decade. If this trend continues, increased reliance on central information processing will place an even greater demand on scalable, fault-tolerant network services.

Network architectures identify the technologies necessary for delivering information and outline the ways that those technologies will be implemented and maintained. At a high level, network architectures encompass the communication needs of all organization members, partners, subsidiaries, and affiliates. They should be used as a tool to help guide the information integration of newly developed partnerships or acquisitions, many of which will require remote services. An architecture would govern what web server hardware/software would be purchased, how network computers would be employed, and how employees would communicate via e-mail with business partners.

Internet investments should be aligned closely with network architectures. Most first-generation Internet solutions provide simple, text-based information and can operate over traditional networks with little or no modification. Although new Internet-based products like voice and video conferencing are quickly entering the market, most healthcare organizations cannot implement these applications without major network upgrades or overhauls. Some organizations may have to accelerate the installation of next-generation networking technology. Large-scale solutions in this category are usually a more long-term, strategic project given the capital expenditures and critical business role this technology will be supporting. Thus, significant lead time will often be required to move forward.

Security Plan

Given the relative ease of exchanging information over the Internet, every organization should have a comprehensive security plan governing information access and supporting technology. A security plan should establish technology standards and operating guidelines for protecting the organization's information assets.

Conclusion

The healthcare issues involving Internet/intranet connectivity are not new. In fact, they have little if anything to do with the Internet in particular. In many ways, Internet-related technology solutions can be evaluated using traditional methods with minor modifications. It is important to limit implementation to only those components that can provide measurable and quantifiable benefits; moreover, the business drivers of the organization should govern their implementation.

Given its potentially significant advantages, the question is not whether the Internet and Internet-related technologies should be used, but rather how their utilization will support the business objectives of the organization. Success is dependent on several fundamental factors. Organizations must

- link Internet needs to business strategy/requirements;
- define the expectations, benefits, and expected outcomes of Internet applications;
- ensure that the sufficient supporting network technology infrastructure is in place to complement the Internet applications or be prepared to invest in such infrastructure; and
- not ignore the importance of training. Sufficient time and money must be allocated to the educational component of implementation, because such an investment affects a large number of people.

The absence of any of these factors will result in the failure of a project. This is true of any IS application, but especially true with regard to the Internet.

9

Issues and Concerns
Briggs Pille and Ed Fulford

The advantages and opportunities offered by Internet technology are not without issues and concerns. The very characteristics of Internet technology that make it revolutionary (e.g., global access, ease of use, and flexibility) are the bases for critical problem areas. These problem areas are common throughout industries and markets, but the healthcare industry has specific concerns.

This chapter will discuss the major issues and concerns from a healthcare perspective. The discussion is theoretical and is not intended to be a technical source. It outlines some of the current methods of addressing and minimizing the concerns regarding Internet usage.[1] In particular, the areas to be addressed are

- security, privacy, and confidentiality;
- reliability and control;
- liability; and
- user acceptance.

Security, Privacy, and Confidentiality

Nearly every conversation about business uses of the Internet is closely followed by a discussion of security. Everyone is concerned about Internet security, and this issue is particularly relevant in a healthcare context. However, it is important to define security, as this term is often used as an umbrella for all privacy-related issues. Privacy is the right of an individual to control disclosure of his or her medical information. Confidentiality is the understanding that medical information will only be disclosed to authorized users at specific times of need. Security includes the processes and mechanisms used to control the disclosure of information.

In healthcare, privacy and confidentiality are critical, regardless of the means used to store and communicate patient information. Even with the manual systems used by many organizations, privacy and confidentiality are far from guaranteed. However, the widespread access offered by the Internet extends these issues beyond the walls of the hospitals, clinics, and physicians' offices. How, then, can a healthcare organization provide privacy and confidentiality when the Internet provides connectivity (but not authorized access) to millions people across the world? This challenge faces any organization wishing to leverage the Internet.

Before we define a security process and identify available security tools, we must understand the threats to privacy and confidentiality. Many security studies have found that as much as 75 percent of all security breaches are internal to an organization.[2] That fact is important to understand when defining a security policy. However, this discussion will focus on external security threats, because they are the additional burden associated with use of the Internet. Threats can be loosely grouped into three major areas, although there are many variations and approaches:

Unauthorized access to servers or databases. This is obtaining access to application or database servers containing confidential information. The intent could be to view, copy, or alter the stored information. Without proper security measures, a "hacker," or a user attempting to violate a system or network, could access patient information in a hospital's core HIS system, perhaps to obtain demographic information or diagnosis information on a celebrity patient.

Unauthorized access to end-user device. This is obtaining access and control of an end-user device (e.g., PC or terminal) with the intent of receiving confidential information or using the device as a "front" to access other secure systems. Security policies and procedures must extend to all points of network access. A classic hacker approach would be to penetrate a less secure location, such as a clinic or physician's office, to eventually access the real target, perhaps a hospital system.

Unauthorized access to network transactions. This is obtaining access to confidential information during transmission. If the Internet is used to transport messages (e.g., e-mail or systems transactions), hackers may attempt to access information such as a lab result that is being transmitted to a physician's office. A successful attempt would obviously compromise patient privacy and confidentiality.

The potential for these threats to a healthcare organization will only increase as the industry moves toward the goal of an electronic patient record across the continuum of care. A breach of security at any point of access could compromise the entire network system.

Security is not a new requirement for information technology. Concerns over unauthorized access to information through automated systems and applications have been voiced from the beginning of the information revolution. However, time and experience have proven that well-designed, implemented, and managed information systems are more secure than the manual processes they replaced. Most people and organizations have become comfortable with IS security within a closed environment, but add the exposure of the worldwide Internet, and faith in existing security measures is quickly lost. In the Internet's highly distributed environment, limits on the effective implementation of physical and administrative controls lead to a greater reliance on security technology. Most organizations are still not comfortable with the security technology offered today.

To make the transition to highly distributed and linked systems easier, healthcare can look to other industries for examples. Financial services and banking may offer the best example. Banks were some of the first businesses to embrace information technology because of the operational cost benefits that could be derived in the high-volume, transaction-oriented banking business. Initially, the incorporation of this technology met with resistance, but that was nothing compared with the reaction when automated teller machines (ATMs) were introduced. ATMs offered many potential benefits for both the bank and the customers, but customers were concerned about security and the safety of their accounts. It took years before ATM technology had widespread acceptance and customers felt comfortable using ATMs as their primary means of banking. Although some people still would rather enter a bank to withdraw money, most people use ATMs on a regular basis.

A similar period of evolutionary acceptance must be expected for Internet technology within healthcare. Most of the technology and tools required to securely operate healthcare ISs in a highly distributed and accessible environment are available today, but it will take time for people to accept and feel comfortable with the solutions.

Common Security Mechanisms

Security was previously described as the processes and mechanisms used to control the disclosure of information. This section will describe those processes in detail and discuss their roles in today's healthcare environment.

Authentication. This is the verification of the claimed identity of a computer or computer user. The technique used to implement this service is referred to as "secure handshaking," a process by which secret information known by both computers is used to validate the establishment of communications between the two systems. Traditional information consists of a user ID and password. Additional information (e.g., random number exchanged during last communication or an algorithm seed) is requested by more advanced systems like Main Line Health System of Philadelphia, which has chosen to use SecureID, a hardware and software product for advanced user authentication. This additional level of authentication provides physicians and remote users with secure access to services and information. More advanced solutions use digital certificates, also known as a digital ID. A digital certificate is the electronic equivalent of a passport, which is issued by a trusted authority (e.g., Verisign). With a digital ID, an individual or organization can present a certificate electronically to prove his or her identity.

Access control. Access control is a service that verifies and enforces the user's authorized access to a computer network after that user's authentication. Techniques used for access control services include access lists, in which a user's identification is related to an access level, and user profiles, in which a user's system privileges and roles for accessing data are specifically defined.

Data integrity. This function verifies that the contents of a message, file, or program have not been changed in an unauthorized manner. Encryption of data communications between computers is a method used to protect data integrity.

Data confidentiality. This service protects against unauthorized disclosure of the information content of data. Encryption of messages or files is one of the techniques that ensure this confidentiality.

Nonrepudiation. Protection against denial of sending or receiving an item containing data is the primary goal of this service. Use of "digital signatures," which use encryption technology to digitally mark a message or file as originating from a specific user, is a key technique for providing nonrepudiation.

Availability. Network communication and connectivity must be maintained to enable users to securely share information. This service helps ensure that the network cannot be compromised by attempts to flood communication links to cut off services. Network management and security administration procedures are often used to maintain service availability.

Beyond basic network and application authentication and access controls, an Internet security process should be based on two key technology tools: a firewall and encryption software.

Firewalls. An Internet firewall is the cornerstone of most Internet security approaches. Nearly all healthcare organizations that have Internet connections have installed a firewall. Not all firewalls are equal, however, nor do they all perform the same functions. There are optional layers of a firewall approach, with two primary firewall architectures available in the market today: packet filtering and application gateway.

Packet filtering, usually performed by a router, provides basic network access control based on protocol information (i.e., rules and conventions necessary for communication between computers). Transmission control protocol (TCP)/Internet protocol (IP) is the communications protocol used on the Internet. The firewall is configured to examine IP packets and filter the packets according to a set of predefined rules. These rules specify the conditions under which packets should be passed through or denied access. One common filter is to limit access based on origination address. If the packet did not come from a known, authorized address, it should not be passed.

Content filtering is increasingly being used for filtering web-based content. Organizations providing users access to Internet information can also prevent access to improper nonbusiness sites (e.g., involving such activities as gambling). Filters, which can be applied on the basis of time of day or user, are usually applied by either web site keyword or site classification. The latter is becoming more popular with healthcare organizations, as keyword filtering often incorrectly masks sites (e.g., preventing a physician from searching breast cancer web sites because of the word "breast").

Application-level gateway front-ends all sessions to the network with a proxy session established by the gateway. The secure session is only established if the user has proper authorization. In this configuration, only the gateway maintains sessions with secured internal hosts. This level of interaction can control access based on applications (e.g., FTP, Telnet, e-mail, HTML), a flexibility that packet-filtering firewalls cannot provide. The secure session is continuously monitored and audit logs are maintained. Application-level gateways are implemented as software on a host platform, which must be configured to avoid penetration of the firewall.

As a host of variations and hybrids of the two major architectures continue to infiltrate the market, a pressing question remains: What is the best solution? Packet filtering is a basic level of security that should always be used. Application-level gateways can provide additional security and flexibility, but these are more complex and require a higher degree of skill to configure and manage. A combination of these architectures provides the greatest degree of security. The most appropriate solution depends on specific requirements and the budget and skills available.

Encryption software. Data and network encryption are also essential components of an Internet security approach. Encryption is the process of translating information into a coded form to prevent unauthorized access. Encryption schemes are often based on public and private keys, or pieces of information required to encrypt and decrypt a message. Only users with the appropriate public and private key can decrypt an encrypted message. Vendors (e.g., Entrust Technologies) are beginning to offer packaged solutions for secure networking over the Internet. These solutions can combine encryption and key/certificate management.

Data encryption is the storage of data in an encoded form to prevent unauthorized access to information stored in a server or database. Network encryption is the encoding of a message or transaction prior to transmitting the message on the network. This prevents unauthorized access during network transmission.

Firewalls and encryption can help address the threats described in the beginning of this chapter. Unauthorized access to servers or databases can be prevented through the use of an Internet firewall, data encryption, or both. Unauthorized access to network transactions is best addressed through the use of network encryption. If a hacker were to intercept a message, he or she would be unable to interpret the lab results or even know that the message contained a lab result. As with most technologies, these security tools are effective only when teamed with proper design, implementation, and management.

Reliability and Control

A technology solution is valuable only if it is reliable and easily controlled. Reliability is the ability to consistently deliver an acceptable level of performance and service. Control is the ability to directly and immediately identify, diagnose, and resolve issues related to performance, reliability, configuration, capacity, and security. Reliability and control may be the main disadvantages to the use of the Internet in healthcare, because market efforts to address reliability and control are lagging behind functionality and security initiatives.

No comprehensive administrative and management structure exists for the Internet. Standards bodies like the Internet Engineering Task Force have been formed to address technical issues and challenges, but no one organization or entity manages the entire Internet. Internet administration and management is a highly distributed function spread across ISPs and a few government and scientific organizations like the National Science Foundation. When a business uses the Internet, no one provider is responsible for all service and performance. A physician in Japan having difficulty accessing a research database at a Florida-based hospital cannot just call his or her ISP and have the problem solved immediately. The problem may involve components or links beyond the control of the ISP. This lack of control is a concern to users as well as service providers.

A hypothetical scenario may better explain the issue of reliability and control. An organization received two responses to a request for proposal for WAN services that would link the entities of an IDS. One proposal offered assurances of performance and reliability, but it carried a high price tag. The second proposal offered a much cheaper solution, but this one could not ensure reliable service and performance. Add to this dilemma a reference or two detailing the second provider's past problems with reliability and performance. Which provider proposal should the organization select?

This hypothetical scenario is not unlike the problem of determining whether to use a private network (potentially an intranet) or try to leverage the Internet. The potential cost savings, flexibility, and speed of implementation are attractive benefits of Internet usage. Because of this, healthcare organizations should carefully consider the requirements of network links when selecting a solution. Links between major entities or locations may require a high degree of reliability and control, and they may be best served by a private connection (e.g., frame relay, T1). Internet connectivity to physician offices, homes, or both may be a more appropriate and cost-effective solution. Healthcare organizations looking to implement or merge into an IDS will need to develop an Internet/intranet staff that will actively manage the components of the Internet/intranet links within their control for the applications selected. This staff will need to develop and enforce such standards as

- quality of service;
- disaster recovery;
- quality (timeliness) of data;
- end-to-end costs; and
- change management.

Any initiatives designed to reach a large, widespread user community would have to include serious consideration of Internet use.

Liability

Another issue linked with Internet use is liability. To what degree is an organization responsible for information provided through its Internet site or for the actions of its employees over the Internet? In healthcare, this issue is especially important, because it deals with life and death. "Ask a Nurse" or "Health Advice" services are becoming popular and useful in today's managed care environment, and the Internet's accessibility and penetration make it a good channel for delivering such services. However, managing the risks associated with these services is essential. Providing inappropriate or easily misunderstood advice could lead to liability issues. This issue exists whether a telephone, private network, or the Internet is used. Proper controls and procedures must be in place to ensure accurate content and usage.

The Telecommunications Act of 1996 addresses the issue of liability, albeit on a limited basis. It does state that "employers are not responsible for actions of employees unless the employee's conduct is within the scope of employment and is known, authorized, or ratified by the employer."[3] Regardless of the legal liabilities involved, most organizations will wish to prevent misuse of facilities for purposes inconsistent with the mission and goals of the organization. Tools are available to report on employee usage and activity, and review processes should be established to watch for inappropriate behavior. The Hospital of Saint Raphael in New Haven, Connecticut, has chosen to use WebSense, a tool that filters and monitors user activity. WebSense will help Saint Raphael preserve the Catholic values of the organization.

User Acceptance

Beyond the security-based user-acceptance issues outlined above, Internet technology is often intimidating. The graphical and interactive nature of the WWW has helped to address this issue but has not resolved it. Most computer-savvy users quickly become comfortable with the web's look and feel and can intuitively navigate the Internet, and this may be fine for automating a mobile sales force or providing research access. People working in healthcare, however, are obviously not all computer-savvy users.

Physicians and other caregivers have spent years learning to care for and treat patients, but not all of them are comfortable with computers. Ease of use and a graphical user interface are not enough for this user community. Internet services provided within an organization must focus on delivering value to the caregivers; services must make their jobs easier or relieve their administrative burden so they can focus on providing care. Once a valuable service is demonstrated and is proven reliable, these users will gradually accept the solution. If this acceptance is not obtained, the expected benefits of the system will never be realized.

Continuing medical education (CME) is one area of opportunity; here, Internet technology can facilitate expanded staff participation and offer a more collaborative environment. A CME initiative of this type will be successful only if the target audience accepts the technology used to deliver the training.

Another healthcare target-user community is the member, patient, or consumer of healthcare services. This community may be the most challenging of all to reach. Improved operating efficiencies mean little to consumers; quality and cost of service are what matter to them. Many managed care organizations are considering the use of the Internet to allow members to check benefits, claim status, or reimbursements. Users with an Internet or other online account could check this information 24 hours a day, seven days a week—but would members actually use the Internet to check this information? They would have to connect to their Internet provider, attach to the managed care company site, log in to the server, access the desired information, log out, and then disconnect from their Internet provider. This process may or may not take as long as a phone call to member services. More importantly, how many members would actually feel comfortable completing this process?

General user acceptance of computer and Internet technology will continue to evolve with the changing demographics of society as the generations of computer-educated consumers grow. Until then, the user acceptance level must be weighed when considering and designing services for end consumers.

All technology solutions have issues and concerns to be managed, and the Internet is no exception. Organizations attempting to leverage Internet solutions should remember three key rules of thumb:

1. Determine when and when not to use the Internet within an organization based on the business needs and requirements of each situation.

2. Establish an environment of technology, people, and processes to minimize the risks associated with these issues and concerns.

3. Factor in a period of evolutionary acceptance to build the comfort level and acceptance of the organization and individual users.

Any healthcare organization investigating the use of the Internet will need to follow these guidelines closely as they wrestle with the issues outlined in this chapter. The task of implementing this technology will become easier, as new tools, techniques, and practices are developed each day to assist in the management of these risks and concerns. The message that organizations should carry with them throughout the implementation process is simple. Although the issues surrounding Internet solutions and implementation may appear to be overwhelming, proper network and application design—along with knowledgeable and experienced project managers—will help ensure a successful Internet project.

Notes

1. Other issues and concerns that focus mainly on applications and uses of the Internet in healthcare are discussed in Chapter 2, "The Role of the Internet in Healthcare Opportunities."

2. For the estimate of 75 percent, see T. W. Madron. 1992. *Network Security in the '90s: Issues and Solutions for Managers.* New York: John Wiley & Sons, Inc., 10. For a more recent assessment of internal threats to security, see F. B. Cohen. 1995. *Protection and Security on the Information Superhighway.* New York: John Wiley & Sons, Inc.

3. A Communications Decency Act of 1996.

Glossary

56K Circuit   Special digital telephone circuits transmit data at 56,000 bits per second. Personal computer modems that operate at this speed have been announced by equipment manufacturers.

Advanced Digital Network (ADN)   The advanced digital network provided by telecom carriers offers services including data rates of 56K and 1.5M bits per second.

AIX   A version of the Unix operating system provided by IBM.

Application Programming Interface (API)   Defines the interaction between two discrete computer programs, such as a client and a server. CGI is also an example of an API. See *Common gateway interface.*

ARPANET   This early shared-use computer network was sponsored by the Advanced Research Projects Agency, an organization of the Department of Defense.

ASCII   The American Standard Code for Information Interchange is a commonly used system for representing printed letters as numbers for processing and storage in computer systems.

Asynchronous transfer mode (ATM)   A very high-speed LAN and WAN protocol that is coming into use for high-capacity segments of the Internet.

Bandwidth   The maximum rate or throughput of a
                             communications circuit. Modems have a
                             bandwidth ranging from 19,200 to 56,000 bits
                             per second. Office video conferencing systems
                             often use T1 circuits at 1,544,000 bits per second.

Bit   A single binary (0 or 1) digit in the internal
                             representation of numbers or text in a computer
                             or communication circuit.

Browser   A personal computer program used to view
                             multimedia web pages created using HTML and
                             possibly including graphics, images, video, and
                             sound. Netscape first became famous for their
                             Navigator browser. Microsoft rapidly improved
                             their browser, Internet Explorer.

Bulletin board   A BBS is usually accessed via dial-up with
system (BBS)   analog modems from a PC to access software
                             libraries, data archives, or e-mail. User groups,
                             vendors, and other businesses or organizations
                             may sponsor a BBS.

Byte   A standard unit of data storage or
                             communications, typically consisting of
                             eight bits.

Call center   Any group of workers using telephones to
                             respond to customer queries or transaction
                             requests, whether the calls are inbound or
                             outbound, and wherever the workers are
                             located, be it at a centralized facility, from
                             multiple sites, or by telecommuting from offices
                             at home.

Chat rooms/chat   Chat rooms are online, real-time, text-based
groups   discussions using the Internet or proprietary
                             providers (e.g., AOL, CompuServe). In
                             proprietary networks these discussions are
                             typically monitored and moderated by an
                             individual employed or contracted by the
                             service provider to ensure acceptable discussion
                             content.

Client   A program that runs on a PC and accesses other
                             network resources, such as a browser.

Common gateway interface (CGI)	An interface definition that a web server may use to interact with other programs on the server or in the network.
Computer telephony integration (CTI)	The use of computer software to coordinate a PC workstation and a telephone. This allows the PC to answer and place calls under software control, and it displays such telephone information as who is calling and length of the call.
Database management system (DBMS)	A program usually run on a server that organizes and stores information for retrieval by specialized client programs.
Demand management	The use of standardized courses of therapy and even scripted advice provided over the phone to augment visits to the doctor's office are key elements of demand management, which aims to achieve lower, more predictable costs. The goal is to provide uniform, quality care with a reduced, predictable cost of delivery.
Digital artist	A professional artist skilled at editing and manipulating photographic images and using computer-based graphics programs to create color schemes, images, designs, and icons.
Domain name	The logical address of an Internet site, such as www.yahoo.com, www.fcgnet.com, www.microsoft.com, or www.netscape.com.
Domain name service (DNS)	A server program that translates names of network resources into numeric TCP/IP addresses.
Electronic data interchange (EDI)	Transfer of business transaction information between organizations over a data communications network. Increasingly, EDI is conducted over the Internet.
E-mail	A personal computer program used to send and receive messages from other computer users, either within an organization or between organizations. E-mail is starting to convey multimedia information, such as audio and images, instead of just simple text.
Ethernet	A widely used LAN protocol that has a bandwidth of 10 million bits per second.

Fast ethernet	An emerging LAN protocol that has a bandwidth of 100 million bits per second.
File transfer protocol (FTP)	A format that provides personal computer users and other computer systems to send and receive files of information over an intranet or the Internet.
Firewall	Computer hardware and software used to restrict the flow of information between a private network or intranet and the Internet to approved individuals and applications. See *Intranet* and *Internet*.
Frequently asked questions (FAQ)	FAQ is a document on an Internet server or in a book that provides answers to common and significant questions in a particular subject area.
Graphical user interface (GUI)	Use of a pointing device or mouse to control a personal computer program as a supplement to the typewriter-style keyboard.
Health Plan Employer Data and Information Set (HEDIS)	A standardized report card for rating health plans on quality, utilization, and satisfaction measures.
Hyper text transport protocol (HTTP)	Governs the transmission of multimedia web pages from a web server to a browser. See *Browser* and *Web*.
Hyper Text Markup Language (HTML)	HTML is the document description protocol used on servers on the WWW. HTML defines fonts, colors, and other format control features.
Integrated delivery system (IDS)	An IDS refers to an organization (typically not-for-profit) that offers a continuum of healthcare services including but not limited to primary care physicians and clinics, urgent care centers, hospitals, multispecialty clinics, long-term care, home health, women's services, and so on. These services are typically offered under one brand name within a local community.
Integrated services digital network (ISDN)	The ISDN is a subset of the public telecom network that uses digital services and standard protocols to transmit voice and data and rates of 56,000 bits per second and greater.

International Telecommunications Union (ITU)	Agency that establishes and publishes some global standards for voice and data communications.
Internet	The collection of linked public and private networks that operate in agreement with rules published by the IETF. See *IETF*. The Internet is a collection of linked networks based on the TCP/IP protocol that grew out of the earlier Arpanet.
Internet Engineering Task Force (IETF)	A computer network working group that develops and publishes standards and procedures for networks that connect with and are part of the Internet.
Internet protocol (IP)	A standard data communications routing protocol used in the Internet that enables an end user to contact, address, or view any publicly available information, server, or computer resource.
Internet service provider (ISP)	Provides shared access to the Internet for individuals, businesses, or other organizations that want to use their computers to connect with the Internet.
Intranet	A private computer network that is constructed using Internet tools and protocols and that is operated consistently with Internet practices.
Java	The Java programming language was developed by Sun Microsystems and is popular for creating programs that can be downloaded over the Internet to run in multiple hardware environments.
Kilobyte (KB)	1,000 bytes.
Leased line	A dedicated or reserved point-to-point communications channel.
Local area network (LAN)	A workgroup, departmental, or site-level network of personal computers and shared computer resources.
Megabyte (MB)	One million bytes.

Modem	A device used to convert a digital data stream into an analog signal that can be sent over an analog telephone line, typically by dialing up an ISP from a PC.
Mosaic	An early web browser that preceded Navigator and Internet Explorer.
National Committee on Quality Assurance (NCQA)	Independent not-for-profit organization that accredits HMOs and prepares "report cards" on HMO quality.
Network computer (NC)	A proposed computer product that is optimized to run a browser and other applications that may be accessed from an Internet or intranet server.
Object linking and embedding (OLE)	A method for sharing or exchanging information between Windows applications.
Packet switching	A data communications method based on chopping large blocks of information, such as files or images, into smaller, easily manageable chunks for transmission over shared communications channels.
Personal computer (PC)	A self-contained computer system, often controlled by a Microsoft Windows, Apple Macintosh, or Unix operating system.
Point of presence (POP)	An access point to a telecom carrier or service, such as the POP for connecting from the local telephone company to a designated long distance carrier.
Point of service (POS)	Managed care plan, combining aspects of both HMO and PPO plans, to reduce costs by managing utilization while providing some choice of medical providers.
Rapid application development (RAD)	Rapid application development emerged as a way to use powerful computer application tools to build software without time-consuming formal analysis and specification procedures. A prototype of the desired application is created very rapidly and is refined through a series of iterative demonstration and critique sessions. RAD is most effective for applications that do not require complex business logic, such as intranet information access.

Router	A data network device used to store and forward data packets between multiple packet switching networks.
Secure access	Use of encryption of the data stream between the browser and web server (https), based on user ID and password, to protect the information from access by unauthorized parties.
Server	A computer or program that is shared by multiple users or clients, often connected by the Internet.
T1	A leased line communications service with a bandwidth of 1.544 million bits per second.
Uniform Resource locator (URL)	The Internet address of a server or information resource, such as www.fcg.com, the URL for the First Consulting Group's web server. See *Web*.
Unix	A computer operating system often used on engineering workstations and high-performance computer servers.
Web application	Any information processing or transaction capability that is delivered over the Internet or intranet from a web server to users with browsers.
Web server	A computer or suite of computers that run software using web protocols (principally http, https, and ftp) to service users with browsers over the Internet or intranet.
Wide area network (WAN)	A computer network that includes more than one physical location, building or facility. Campus networks and metropolitan networks may be viewed as wide-area networks for the purpose of understanding the Internet.
Workstation	Typically refers to a personal computer controlled by the Unix operating system. May also refer to an extremely large or powerful personal computer.
World Wide Web (WWW or Web)	That portion of the Internet that stores and exchanges multimedia information using the hyper text transport protocol. See *HTTP*.

Index

Contributors

Dean Arnold is a director for First Consulting Group (FCG) with a specialization in communications technology and enterprise computing. His background includes more than ten years of extensive experience in planning, design, and implementation for systemwide information networks in the healthcare environment. Mr. Arnold has recently been involved in several client engagements that have made extensive use of Internet/intranet technologies both in the United States and Europe. Prior to working at FCG, Mr. Arnold was a communications engineer for Electronic Data Systems, designing and managing the implementation of several of their large-scale communication networks. Mr. Arnold received a BS in computer information systems from Clemson University.

Steve Ditto is a vice president in the Network Integration practice of FCG. During the past 14 years, he has focused on providing consulting services on networking and telecommunications issues for a variety of healthcare clients with a primary focus on providing strategic planning, design, and implementation management services for larger healthcare provider and managed care organizations. During the last three years, Mr. Ditto has assisted several large IDS and managed care clients in identifying Internet-based strategies for enhancing customer relationships with healthcare consumers. Mr. Ditto received a BS in electrical engineering from Vanderbilt University.

Ed Fulford has more than 13 years of experience in information technology, telecommunications, and security. He has been a manager in the network security and business continuity planning practice with leading international CPA and consulting firms. He has had additional experience as the network security and fraud control manager for a global telecommunications joint venture. Mr. Fulford has spoken widely on the topics of network, Internet, and telecommunications security, and is an active member of the International Information Systems Security Certification Consortium and the National Association of Certified Fraud Examiners. He holds a BS in business administration from the University of Florida and an MBA from Troy State University.

Aaron Garinger specializes in information technology, strategic planning, selection, and tactical operations for healthcare information systems. His experience includes commercial planning for community health information networks (CHINs), reengineering of clinical systems, strategic Internet planning, and system selections. Additionally, he has gained specialized expertise in emerging healthcare Internet offerings, including the areas of infrastructure and content. He is a member of the Healthcare Information and Management Systems Society, Health Level 7, and the Microsoft Healthcare Users Group. Mr. Garinger received his BS in General Management and Finance from Purdue University.

Kent Gray is a senior manager in FCG's Network Integration Services service line. With more than eight years of healthcare networking experience, he has led numerous network assessment, design, and implementation engagements for organizations across the country. He currently shares responsibility for managing FCG's Internet Services area of expertise. Mr. Gray holds both an aerospace engineering degree and a master of science management degree from the Georgia Institute of Technology. Prior to working at FCG, he managed network and customer support services for a 350-bed medical center in Atlanta. Mr. Gray is currently leading several Internet/intranet projects in the Northeast, which include web assessment, Internet strategy planning, and web services development.

Peter Kilbridge is a clinical practice specialist master with ten years of experience. He has developed physician integration strategies for multiple enterprises, assisted large academic medical centers with clinical applications architecture, and led an FCG study of best practices for information management at ten leading integrated delivery networks. His professional affiliations include the American Medical Informatics Association (AMIA), the American College of Healthcare Executives (ACHE), and the Association of Medical Directors of Information Systems. Dr. Kilbridge received an AB from Harvard University and an MD from Case Western Reserve University.

Louis Nicholson is a vice president in FCG's Houston office and has 28 years of communication and technology consulting experience within the healthcare industry. Mr. Nicholson joined FCG in 1987 and founded what has evolved into its Advanced Technology Practice. He has been a leading proponent for the integration of network applications and technology into the planning, design, selection, and implementation of enterprise-based healthcare information architectures and systems. In addition to having provided technology consulting services to virtually hundreds of community and academic medical center clients during his career, Mr. Nicholson has also worked extensively with many of the country's leading integrated delivery systems and networks.

John Odden is practice director in the Advanced Technology Group in FCG's Los Angeles office. Mr. Odden joined FCG in 1996, bringing 18 years' experience in telecommunications, data processing, and healthcare, including ten years in a variety of management roles with a major telecom equipment manufacturer. His clients include major HMOs, teaching hospitals, and insurance companies. His project experience covers call center architecture, design and implementation, specification of interactive voice response applications, voice network design, and broadband network migration. He prototyped several call center applications that employ Internet and intranet technology to achieve simplified user access and rapid development timelines. Mr. Odden holds a BS in mathematics from the California Institute of Technology and has studied at the Harvard Business School. He is a member of the Microsoft Healthcare User Group.

Briggs Pille is a Director for FCG specializing in enterprise networks and distributed computing. He has more than ten years of network and system architecture, design, and implementation experience. Mr. Pille has more than five years of healthcare-specific experience with major IDSs, academic medical centers, and alternate site providers. He has recently completed several enterprise network architectures including the integration of Internet and intranet technology. Mr. Pille leads FCG's Internet Technologies area of expertise. He received a BS in computer science and physics from Butler University.

Michael Schneider is a manager for FCG focusing on Clinical Informatics and Operations Effectiveness strategies. He has more than ten years of experience in healthcare. Prior to working at FCG, he directed Internet-related healthcare projects for four years. He has presented numerous lectures and workshops on ways that physicians can use the Internet effectively. He is a member of AMIA and the AMIA Internet Working Group. In addition to his work with FCG, Dr. Schneider is a board-certified anesthesiologist and an assistant clinical professor at the University of California Irvine College of Medicine. Dr. Schneider received his BA in zoology at Duke University and his MD from Case Western Reserve University School of Medicine.

Paul Steinichen has ten years of experience engineering the collection and communication of data and information in a variety of industries. His current interests lie in the communication of information throughout the healthcare integrated delivery network using a combination of object-oriented, web browser, and expert agent technologies. Mr. Steinichen leads the Shared Network Services interest group within FCG. He lives in New Smyrna Beach, Florida, where he enjoys remodeling his house when he is not tapping his Toshiba.

Maria Sundeen is a freelance journalist based in Southern California. In the last ten years, she has published numerous books and articles and conducted research on topics ranging from nuclear disarmament to trade and healthcare policy. She is a member of the Society of Professional Journalists and has assisted in the production of various technology, business, and political programs with CNN, C NET, the BBC, and others. Ms. Sundeen holds a BA in journalism and master's degrees in policy studies and French studies from the Monterey Institute of International Studies.

Tim Webb, a vice president for FCG's Integration Services, is responsible for client engagements addressing information integration and information architectures. He has 15 years of experience in designing and implementing applications and network and database technology to address business needs in various industries, ten of them in healthcare. Specific projects he has performed related to intranet tools have included Internet strategies for health plans and healthcare delivery systems. He is a member of the Institute of Electrical and Electronics Engineers, Inc. (IEEE) and Healthcare Information and Management Systems Society (HIMSS). Mr. Webb received his BS in electrical engineering from Purdue University.